Osprey AutoHistory

FORD MUSTANG

1965-70; Hardtop, Convertible, Fastback; 6 & V8

F. WILSON McCOMB

Published in 1983 by Osprey Publishing Limited
12-14 Long Acre, London WC2E 9LP
Member company of the George Philip Group

Sole distributors for the USA

Osceola, Wisconsin 54020, USA

British Library Cataloguing in Publication Data

McComb, F. Wilson
    Ford Mustang.—(Osprey authohistory series)
    1. Mustang automobiles.
    I. Title
    629.2′222   Tl215.M8

ISBN 0-85045-504-9

Editor Tim Parker
Associate Michael Sedgwick
Picture research by the author

Filmset in Great Britain
Printed in Spain
by Grijelmo S.A. Bilbao

Contents

The Mustang concept

The advertisements in American magazines—magazines that we in Europe once found so fascinatingly different from our own—used to include, I remember, a series plugging some kind of piano lessons. I forget the details apart from the headline, which was 'They laughed when I sat down to play...' We laughed until it hurt when Ford USA first sat down to play at European-style motor sport in the early 1960s, for their initial approach was so hopelessly wrong. All right, they beat the Jaguars in saloon car racing during 1963; they damn well should, with engines that were nearly twice the size in those huge Galaxies raced by 'Gentleman Jack' Sears, Sir Gawaine Baillie and others. But in the Falcon Sprint team's first Monte Carlo Rally, they didn't get one car into the top thirty.

That was in 1963, and if anyone had told us that before the decade was over Dearborn would win Le Mans four times running *and* back the most successful Grand Prix engine of all time, we would have dismissed it as just the kind of Yankee ballyhoo that Europeans find hardest to swallow. Mind you, they did it with a little help from their friends—in Europe.

Most people have now forgotten that when Ford USA turned to rallying, the Russians were also trying to get in on the act (and their efforts, believe me, *really* brought tears to the eyes). But whereas the Russians accepted failure and quietly trundled back home again in their laughable, lumbering Moskvitches and Volgas, the Americans stayed put and paid attention. They found

Mustang's first big success in European motor sport came when Peter Procter (DPK 7B) and Peter Harper (DPK 6B) took first and second places in the Touring Category of the 1964 Tour de France

DPK 6B reappeared in the 1965 Monte Carlo Rally, driven by Bo Ljungfeldt and Fergus Sager, but was not among the finishers

out why European cars, unlike their own Detroit products, had brakes that worked and suspension systems that allowed fast cornering. They hired European technicians to sort out their cars, and European drivers who knew how to make good use of them. The fact is, Americans learn fast. There are footprints on the moon to prove it.

So the 1964 Monte was a somewhat different ball game. Eight highly-modified Falcons were entered, with drivers such as Graham Hill, Peter Harper, Bo Ljungfeldt and Henri Greder. The timed sections in the mountains were practised for weeks on end, under the control of a lavishly-equipped command team, and even the support cars had 'name' drivers hired for the occasion; it was rumoured that Dearborn's outlay on this one rally exceeded Ford of Britain's competitions budget for an entire year. The betting before the event

was that unless it snowed heavily, the big Fords would pull it off.

It didn't snow heavily, and they damn nearly did. I have reason to remember, for it was my first event as press officer to the British Motor Corporation's competitions department. I stood on the front at Monte Carlo beside our competitions manager, Stuart Turner (now Director of Motorsports, Ford Europe), as results of the five mountain stages came through. Ljungfeldt was fastest on all five with the 260-cube Falcon, but Paddy Hopkirk's ridiculous 65 cubic inches of Mini-Cooper had equalled his time on one, and stayed mighty close on the others—so close, a French colleague told me, that the Mini's 5 per cent handicap allowance would put it in the lead. You will never get Stuart to admit it, but he didn't believe me when I told him this.

On handicap, Ljungfeldt's Ford dropped to fifth

Henri Greder tried hard in the 1966 Monte and finished well up the list, but his Mustang was disqualified that year, along with the British Mini-Coopers

9

After their debut in European rallying, the Mustang team cars led a full life as racers. Here, DPK 6B is seen at Brands Hatch in 1968

overall until the final three-lap scratch race, in which the Swede flung his big Falcon (later referred to by Henry Manney of *Road & Track* as 'a gorgeous great fiberglass mutha') around the Monaco GP circuit to such effect that he pulled right up to second place overall. Thus the Mini won the Monte, and as we of BMC took five more internationals that year, in September we approached the Tour de France with some confidence that we'd beat the Fords again. In 1963, Paddy's Mini-Cooper had stayed with the 3.8-litre Jaguars and even bigger 427-cube (7-litre) Ford Galaxies to come third on scratch, first on handicap, in the Touring category of this extraordinary event, which consisted of ten whole days and 3600 miles of speed tests at some of the best-known European circuits. And if BMC didn't do it, what the hell: the scratch winner of the Touring category in 1960, 1961, 1962 and 1963 had been Bernard Consten's Jaguar, and there was no reason to suppose he wouldn't win it again.

Whatever BMC did on the 1964 Tour de France, it was so very bad that there is a Freudian blank in my memory, though I followed the event from start to finish. We won nothing at all. And there *was* a reason why Consten didn't win the Touring category—in fact two reasons, so he came third. The two reasons were called Mustang, and they were driven by Peter Procter and Peter Harper. No doubt about it—the Americans were learning.

In fact they dropped out of European rallying after the Tour to concentrate on pure racing, and after the Galaxies had shamed the Jaguars in British saloon car racing in 1963/64, Roy Pierpoint's Mustang took the Championship title in 1965. After that the Falcons performed well at this game, and we in Europe saw little of the Mustangs. But Ford USA had made their point: they could win with their cars when they put their minds to it, as they proceeded to demonstrate again at Indianapolis, Le Mans, and the Grand Prix circuits of the world.

It was a remarkable change of image for Dearborn, and just what was wanted by the remarkable young man who, in November 1960, had become head of Ford Division at the age of 36. Lido Anthony Iacocca was the son of an immigrant Italian, though he preferred to be called Lee and pronounced his surname with four syllables (which sounds more Iranian than Italian). He was convinced that Ford needed to move fast to attract younger buyers, for his predecessor, Robert McNamara, had over-reacted to the flamboyant ugliness of 1950s styling by (as *Special Interest Autos* expressed it) 'putting Fords in plain brown wrappers'. They appealed to older people than those who bought Chevrolets, and the difference was accentuated early in 1960 when GM brought out the successful 'Monza' coupé, which soon accounted for threequarters of all Corvair sales.

Just about this time, however, the new American president, John F. Kennedy, invited McNamara to

For Lee Iacocca, the success of the Mustang concept led eventually to presidency of the Ford Motor Company—until his resignation and move to Chrysler in 1978, after a row with Henry Ford II

Above *Styling chief Gene
Bordinat checks a full-sized
'clay' which, like several
experimental Mustangs, had
an upswept front bumper*

Right *First seen in October
1962, the Mustang I prototype
was a sophisticated, mid-
engined two-seater powered by
a 1½-litre V4 unit*

It is obvious that the production Mustang was based on this clay of August 1962—but Joe Oros always preferred the name of Cougar

become his Defence Secretary, leaving Iacocca with the freedom and power to instigate a new Ford Division marketing policy. Research had shown that the post-WW2 'baby boom' would bring a 40 per cent increase in the 15-to-29 age group during the 1960s, and it was estimated that more than half of all new-car sales during the decade would be to buyers between the ages of 18 and 34. For the first time, there would be more Americans aged under 25 than over, and with personal income rapidly increasing, these would be people who had money to spend.

Iacocca aimed to take a substantial slice of that money by offering the eager young buyers a new Ford car they would find irresistible. But first he had to see what there was in the parts bin, and seemingly it didn't amount to much. The previous 'sporting' Ford, the two-seater Thunderbird, had grown into a fat, up-market five-seater. The Falcon, a 'compact' by Detroit standards although it looked as big as a truck to European eyes, had such a non-sporting image that Iacocca's attempt to turn it into a Monte winner was glumly described by one Ford executive as 'putting falsies on Grandma'. Karl Ludvigsen, later a vice-president of Ford Europe but at that time with General Motors in America, summed up Ford's situation to me with his usual discernment: 'From our viewpoint, what Ford did was to make a cheapie version of our Monza coupé; that was the car that pioneered the idea of a sporty small car with bucket seats and a floor shift. Don't forget, the Mustang follows closely on the heels of the compact revolution, and without the compacts there would never have been a Mustang. First we had the upheaval when the new generation of small cars came on the market, something Detroit had never built before. Once they existed, there was the temptation to make sporty cars out of them. The Corvair didn't need much modification to do that, but Ford had the dull-as-ditchwater Falcon and had to make a totally different car out of that; the Mustang would never have been financially viable but for the fact that it used Falcon and Fairlane components.

'What we at GM didn't grasp, or grasped belatedly, was that with the conventional powertrain of the Mustang, as distinct from our exotic, air-cooled flat six, they were able to offer an incredibly wide range of engines, gearboxes, power packs, trim levels, etc. That was quite a feat, to make a base car with the capability of being dressed up, powered up, fixed up in so many ways to suit so many different buyers. *That* is the extra dimension Ford added to the concept that GM really pioneered. That, I think, is what made the Mustang

Joe Oros was the man whose design got the go-ahead for development into the production Mustang

15

much more than the Corvair could have been at the time.'

Ludvigsen also commented on the crucial question: two seats or four? 'Nobody viewed the Thunderbird with a sporty image. Well, maybe with the original two-passenger Thunderbird they were groping for the European-style sports car, but in those days nobody really knew what the hell they wanted. Detroit trying to do a European-type car—it was difficult then and it's still difficult today. They thought there was something in this new-fangled two-seat car business, but they weren't quite sure what. Lew Crusoe, who was the guy running Ford Division at the time of the two-seat Thunderbird, took one home before they were announced and when he brought it back, he said: "This would be a great car if it had a back seat." The idea of a four-passenger Thunderbird was born before the two-seat was even launched, because they knew they could do better commercially with a four. The fact that the Mustang was a four-passenger car was vital.' Another American writer has put it this way: 'Fact one: the two-seater design is very popular, especially with the young. Fact

Resemblance between running horse and prancing horse was not entirely accidental: in 1963, Ford had tried unsuccessfully to buy Ferrari

16

two: even young car-buyers often have a family to transport, making the two-seater car impractical. Conclusion: build a car that looks like a two-passenger sports model, but actually has a rear seat. Enter the 1964 Mustang, available as a hardtop or a convertible. In terms of basic styling, the Mustang was comparable to those early two-seater Thunderbirds, yet it had a back seat.'

As it happens, the first car to bear the name of Mustang *was* a two-seater, though the stylist who worked on it says he called it after the WW2 fighter plane of that name, not the Spanish-blooded *mestengo* of the American plains. 'Mustang I' was a highly-advanced, mid-engined V4 derived from a McNamara-inspired economy car called the Cardinal, which eventually turned into Ford of Germany's 12-M Taunus. Dedicated

The pre-production show car called Mustang II is driven by Iacocca, with Graham Hill as his passenger, at a preview in October 1963

17

sports car enthusiasts went crazy over the prototype when Dan Gurney demonstrated it at Watkins Glen in October 1962, but Iacocca knew it was unsuitable for large-scale production; it was given the thumbs-down, and is now seen as the parent of the Le Mans-winning GT40. There were many, many other prototypes which came under consideration, whether as clays or complete motor-cars, with names like Median, Allegro, Stiletto, XT-Bird and so on. As time was beginning to run short, Gene Bordinat, Ford's styling vice-president, instructed several of the company's design studios to compete against each other for Iacocca's approval. The chosen design, by Joe Oros and Dave Ash, was a car called Cougar with a jungle cat running left-to-right in the middle of its front grille. The styling changed but little in

its progress from clay model to production car, but at various times it was known as T5, Special Falcon, Torino, Turino, and even 'Mustang II', a name that was also given to a second running prototype seen at Watkins Glen in late 1963.

So much time went into styling that there was barely enough left to engineer the car, and to do it the project team had to break nearly every rule in the book of correct Ford in-house procedures. In the midst of this high-pressure exercise one of the top brass of Ford announced that he wanted to drive the new car, and a development engineer proudly brought him the team's very best prototype. After a short drive, he said grimly: 'This thing is nothing but a buckboard, and nobody is going to buy it.'

In production form—the original Mustang convertible of early 1964

Fortunately for Iacocca—who had staked some $65 million of Ford money on the Mustang project by this time—continuing market research said otherwise. At an early stage he had stipulated that the new car must weigh under 2500 lb and cost not more than $2500, reckoning it had to be acceptable to the public at less than a dollar a pound. As it turned out, the basic production car weighed 2562 lb but price was held down to just $2368, making it 92 cents a pound! When Ford played the old trick of inviting people to guess the price after seeing a late prototype, the average guess was $3500 to $3800. In one study, fifty-two couples with school-age children said they liked the car but considered it impractical for people like themselves; their estimate of the price was, as usual, about $1000 too high. When told the Mustang would be sold at $2368, they took another look at the car and came up with various excuses to justify buying one for themselves, kids or no kids.

The launching of the Mustang was a publicity man's dream, adding $10 million to the sum already invested in the car, 'to embed it in the national consciousness like a gumdrop in a four-year-old's cheek', said *Newsweek*. Both *Newsweek* and *Time* ran cover stories. There were features in nearly three thousand major newspapers and magazines in the USA alone. Invited pressmen were shown the Mustang at a preview of Ford's exhibit at the New York World's Fair on April 13, 1964, then drove 750 miles to Detroit in a fleet of the new cars. Three days later, nearly thirty million Americans got the chance to see the Mustang in their own homes, for Ford had bought the prime 9.0 pm to 10.0 pm TV commercial time from all three of the top networks: ABC, CBS and NBC. Somewhere in Thief River Falls, Minnesota, there may have been an octogenarian grandmother who didn't know that Ford had brought out a new sporty compact car, but the kids would have told her about it before the month was out.

CHAPTER TWO

Horse to water

People who know about horses tell me you can lead them to water but you can't make them drink, and I found out long ago that you can't make them run fast by piling money on their backs. It is also true that an automobile manufacturer cannot force people to buy cars they don't want, as Ford learned to the tune of $250 million with the Edsel, and British Leyland discovered twenty years later with the Triumph TR7, at a cost of some £80 million.

In this early publicity shot, the polo player not only stresses the equine connection, but also plugs the up-market image that Ford wanted to establish for the Mustang

Early Mustangs aroused considerable interest in Britain. At Dagenham wharf, British Ford employees are almost taking this 1964 model apart

There was the possibility that Ford had got it wrong in a different way with the Mustang. This was a gut-twisting prospect for Iacocca, for if there is one thing worse than designing a car that flops, it is designing one that succeeds, and then not being able to build enough of them. Moreover, the production arrangements have to be settled before the customers have so much as seen the car, which is why big businessmen get ulcers. 'You have to make up your mind,' says Iacocca. 'You can't go home and ask your wife.' Starting with a build estimate of 75,000 for the first year, he had kept increasing this figure during 1963 until eventually he had committed three separate factories to Mustang assembly.

American thinking is very much a product of the sheer size of the country; something we Europeans—and

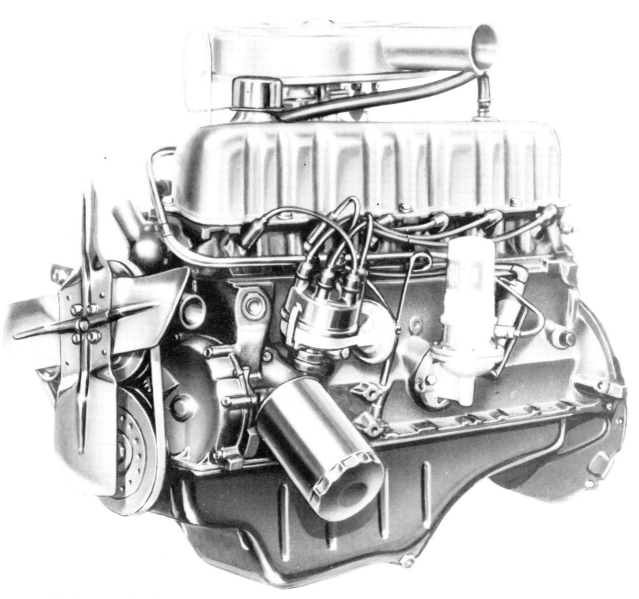

'Exciting as a dish of
babyfood', said Car & Driver
of the 170 cubic inch Falcon
engine for the base-model
Mustang Six. It gave 101 bhp

Ford Mustang Hardtop with Vinyl-Covered Roof

Presenting the unexpected... new Ford Mustang! $2368*

Ford Mustang Convertible

FORD

Above 1965 and the hardtop in white(?). Studio shots were cleverly stage managed to highlight the trim and body pressings

Opposite In their October 1971 issue, Motor Trend showed how Ford's Mustang always outsold the ponycars of GM, Chrysler, Pontiac and AMC, but did not maintain its early record-breaking sales

especially those of us who live in Britain—have never really grasped. You could drop forty Great Britains into the USA and still have 83,227 square miles left over for parking lots. No wonder our cars look as ridiculous in America as American cars do in our country. Our Morris Minor was rated a big hit when it sold 100,000 in the first three-and-a-half years, and one million in just over twelve years. Ford sold 100,000 Mustangs in the first four *months*, and a million in only two years.

Once the wraps were off, nobody had any doubt about the car's success, and Ford dealers now vie with each other to tell stories about that April weekend in 1964: how an estimated four million people flocked to their showrooms before Monday morning, bought every Mustang in sight, and ordered another 22,000 without so much as a demo run. How one dealer had to lock his

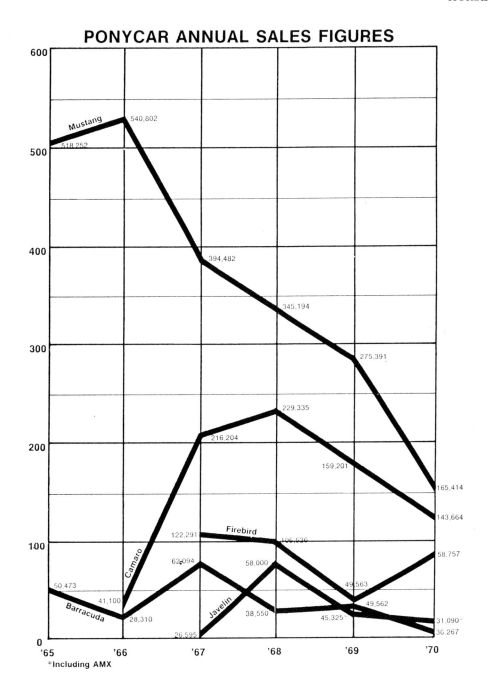

PONYCAR ANNUAL SALES FIGURES

*Including AMX

Mustangs for 1967 were much longer and wider than the original version, and the wider track improved the handling

doors to keep out the crowds in case they wrecked the place, and another put a Mustang on his lube lift, then couldn't get it down again because there were so many people around. How a mesmerized driver put his truck through a showroom window as he gazed at the Mustang inside. How a Texas dealer auctioned off his last Mustang to a bunch of would-be buyers, and the highest bidder slept in the car until his cheque was cleared. Ford had a hard time catching up with the demand. Initially, the only two engines available were a 170 cubic inch six-cylinder and a 260-cube V8. So many chose the V8 that supplies of the bigger engine began to run dry, and Ford's advertising agency, J. Walter Thompson, was told to get young women interested in the six-cylinder Mustang. They did it with a campaign headed 'Six and the Single Girl', and Americans still think of the base-model Mustang as the Secretary Six.

The first Mustang advertisements—and of course it

The 1969 Mach I, like the other 1969 models, was longer and wider again

was Lee Iacocca who told JWT what they should be—were magnificently simple: a bold side-view of a vinyl-roof hardtop with whitewalls, a couple in evening dress, and just half-a-dozen words of splash copy—'Presenting the unexpected . . . new Ford Mustang! $2368'. The detail copy said: 'This is the car you never expected from Detroit. Mustang is so distinctively beautiful it received the Tiffany Award for Excellence in American Design . . . the first time an automobile has been honored with the Tiffany Gold Medal. Mustang has the look, the fire, the flavour of the great European road cars. Yet it's as American as its name.' Readers were told the whitewalls cost an extra $33.90, the vinyl roof another $75.80: 'The basic Mustang is an eminently practical and economical car, yet it was designed to be designed by you. You can make your Mustang into a luxury or high performance car by selecting from a large but reasonably priced group of options.' Naturally, few buyers settled for the Plain Jane model. Usually they added at least $600 in options which brought handy additional profits to Dearborn. Even the middle-aged American mothers who fell for the new Ford, trading in their traditional middle-aged American mothers' station wagons for a Mustang, tended to fall for the options as well. 'My sons refer to it as Ma's mill with four on the floor and eight up front,' wrote one of them, 'I've no idea what they're talking about, but the car sounds as good as it looks.'

It was an essential part of the Mustang's appeal in its own land that it was American, even if the glamour of imported goods was acknowledged with the subtle reference to 'great European road cars'. The Mustang was as American as a hamburger—not the nausea-inducing mess that goes by that name in Britain, but the delicious native product. And like the hamburger, the Mustang offered honest-to-goodness value, whether the buyer chose the simplest version available or a top-dollar carnival with onion, pickle, salad, mayonnaise, catsup, whatever.

Perhaps the saddest man in America at this time was

Simone ('Bunkie') Knudsen, hired from GM in February 1968, campaigned for higher-performance Mustangs and inspired the Boss models

29

John Bond, the amiable publisher of *Road & Track*. Early in 1964 he decided, after years of longing, that the time had come to indulge himself with a brand-new, blood-red 330GT Ferrari. Not too long afterwards, a caller saw it parked outside the office, glanced at the prancing horse symbol and said casually: 'Oh, is that one of those new Mustangs you've got?'

Every source I have consulted gives different sales figures for the Mustang, whether by model year or calendar year, but it is clear that sales of 1965 and 1966 models exceeded the million, even though the 2 + 2 fastback was not available until almost six months after the hardtop and convertible. Alas, it is equally clear that for some reason the Mustang's early level of sales was not maintained; perhaps that would have been an impossible dream, as it constituted a new all-time record for the sale of any American car, whether sporty, compact or bread-and-butter. Whatever the reason, the Mustang attracted fewer buyers every year from 1966/67 to 1973/74.

Opposite *Though it filled the engine compartment to overflowing, the big 429 unit did not match up to a good 428-cube in terms of real performance*

Below *From the car's inception until 1970, annual changes to the Mustang and additions to the model range were made without altering the 108-inch wheelbase.*

1965

1966

1967

1968

1969

1970

It is true that when Chevrolet produced the Camaro, sales of the rival GM ponycar rose as fast as the Mustang's fell, but this is far from being the whole story: the Mustang still outsold the Camaro, which in its very best year did not achieve half the sales of the peak Mustang period. As for Chrysler's Barracuda, Pontiac's Firebird and AMC's Javelin, they were nowhere by comparison, only the Pontiac ever making it over the 100,000 mark for a model year.

So although Mustang sales headed downwards, it remained the best-seller. Things changed, though. An analysis of what might be called the 'soft option' sales shows how the Mustang buyer's tastes altered. Just over half wanted automatic transmission at first, but almost threequarters of them chose it in 1970, and by 1972/3 it was preferred by more than 90 per cent. Less than a quarter originally chose power steering, but almost three times as many buyers specified it in 1970, and again, in a couple more years it was the choice of more than 90 per cent. Not 10 per cent wanted air conditioning in 1965; it was chosen by three times as many customers in 1970, and that proportion doubled in the next two or three years.

The first major change in the car itself came with the 1967 model, which was two inches longer overall, almost three inches wider and more than 130 lb heavier, though most people thought the wider track and new tyres made for better handling. Another big jump in size came for 1969, with the four-headlamp 'Stang which was almost six inches longer than the original, and wider and heavier again to accommodate one of the biggest Ford engines, on the instructions of ex-GM man Bunkie Knudsen. It was not a move that met with everyone's approval, even at Dearborn. 'If we hadn't gone nuts and put the big Boss 429 engine in, the car never would have grown in size.' said Iacocca himself. Mike Lamm, when editor of *Special Interest Autos*, commented: 'I've driven quite a few early Mustangs, and they've always impressed me as being an ideal size, not too big and not to small. The car fits. Ford certainly hit the 'personal' nail dead center, and that's where the later Mustangs missed. They were all too big.'

A few years later, Tim Howley shared his view in *Old Cars*: 'Ford tried hard to recapture its youth market with the '69, '70 and '71 models with their monster engines. But the sheer size of the later Mustangs fought the whole reason for their initial popularity. America loved its little upstart Mustang, and the bigger it got the more the purists turned back to the original.' Some years later still, Bill McBride was to write in the same magazine: 'As the 1970s unfolded, it became clear . . . that the Mustang was getting too big, too long, too fat, too gimmicked up for its well-earned reputation. The design of the car from the beginning meant a serious weight problem on the front end, a problem the engineers never truly solved, though they tried mightily. Even as late as 1971 the Mustang ads claim 'improved handling' as a selling point. But nothing would really do, save a complete redesign. Before that could happen, the 1973 gas crisis put a merciful end to the Mustang in its original, if by then sadly bloated, form.'

Obviously, opinions differ as to the cut-off point for the 'real Mustang'. It seems to me there is a strong case for making it 1970. In the fall of that year the size of the Mustang exploded yet again, and this time to the extent that the wheelbase had to be increased together with the track, length, width, weight and everything else (except the height). It was also the year in which Mustang met Muskie, the Maine senator who pushed through a five-year leap in the Clean Air regulations which effectively strangled the internal combustion engine in America. What this meant in practice was that within a year or so, the hottest engine you could buy for your (bigger, fatter, heavier) Mustang gave fewer horses than the top-of-the-line High-Performance 289-cube of 1964—and what hell use is a Mustang without any horses? For those of us who enjoyed performance, it was time to stay home and read old magazines.

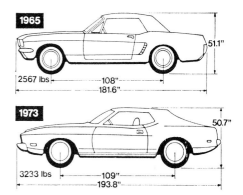

Comparing profiles, the 1973 Mustang is more than a foot longer than the 1965 model. It was also heavier by 666 pounds

CHAPTER THREE

'Stang '65/'66

Officially there is no such thing as a 1964 Mustang, although something around a quarter-million were sold between April and September of that year, before the true 1965 model appeared. Ford like to refer to the pre-1965 model as 'first of the '65s', but nowadays it is usually known as the $1964\frac{1}{2}$. Its existence complicates the production and sales figures, and helps to keep 'Stang enthusiasts arguing whether any Mustang had a DC generator or non-adjustable passenger seat, and if there was ever a V8 with 13-inch wheels.

Structurally, the Mustang was quite a novelty for the USA with its welded-up punt or platform-type chassis which relied mainly on its transmission tunnel and box-section sills (in US parlance, rocker rails) for rigidity. This carried running gear that was either identical or very similar to that of the Falcon, Fairlane and other Ford passenger cars, causing *Car and Driver* to comment: 'It's easily the best thing to come out of Detroit since the 1932 V-8 Model B roadster. But for all Ford's talk of Total Performance, it's still clear that the Mustang has been designed and built to a price.' Which of course it had been, like almost every other car in history. The combination of a platform chassis and mass-produced components was, in fact, exactly the recipe that had been followed for a decade and more in the design of cheap British sports cars like the humble Sprite and other more exalted models. It was a build policy that paid dividends, and a perfectly sound one if the individual components were chosen with care. That, of

Top *To the US auto industry in 1964, the platform-type chassis was a novelty*

Below *Well-placed insulation limited the noise level inside the hardtop model*

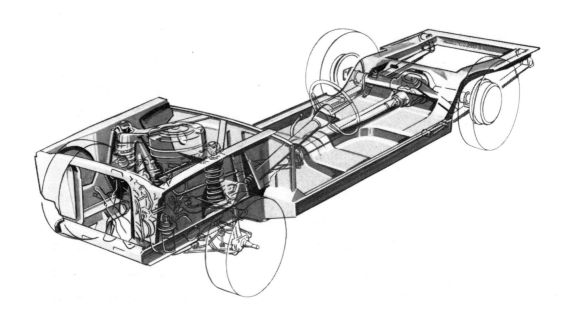

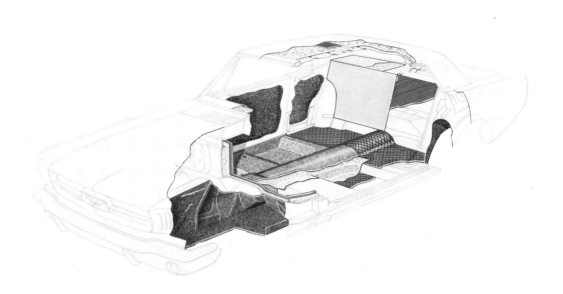

course, was the $64,000 (or in the case of the Mustang, $2368) question.

Front suspension was pure Falcon: an upper wishbone or A-bracket, a single lower arm and trailing control rod, and above the A-bracket a coil spring enclosing the telescopic shock; there was also an anti-sway bar. At the rear the Falcon leaf springs were slightly beefed-up for the Mustang, but they alone located the live axle, which seemed a tightwad approach to rear-end design. This was even more true of the brakes: 9 in. Falcon drums on the Six and 10 in. Fairlane drums on the V8s. It is difficult to make a direct comparison with European practice because at this time most European saloons and certainly every sports car had disc brakes on the front wheels, at least, but the Rover 2000, for example, had the

Front suspension, in standard form, was pure Ford Falcon

same swept area *with its back brakes only* as the Mustang Six had with all four brakes!

At 108 inches the original Mustang was, surprisingly, some six inches longer in the wheelbase than the original Thunderbird, but barely a quarter-inch longer overall. Both had the same track (tread) front and rear, and the two cars were the same width, but the Mustang was half-an-inch lower and the frontal area had been reduced by a fraction; to achieve this, Ford had dropped the height of the Falcon radiator and air-cleaner before ever the Mustang was announced. As a hardtop the Mustang weighed 179 lb less than it did as a convertible, partly because the open car's frame had extra stiffening to compensate for the lack of a roof section. In Plain Jane form the engine was the 170-cube/101 bhp (2.8 litre)

Apart from beefed-up springs, the rear suspension was also taken from the Falcon sedan

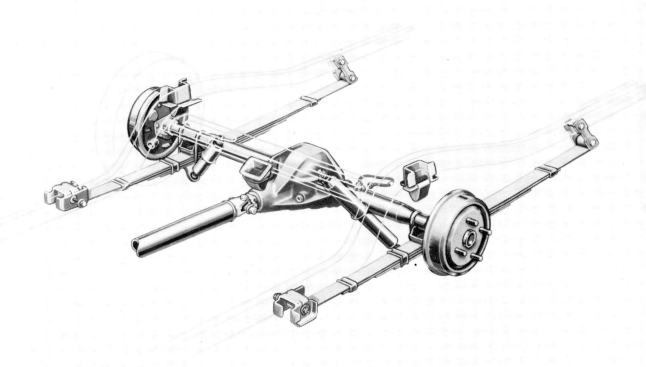

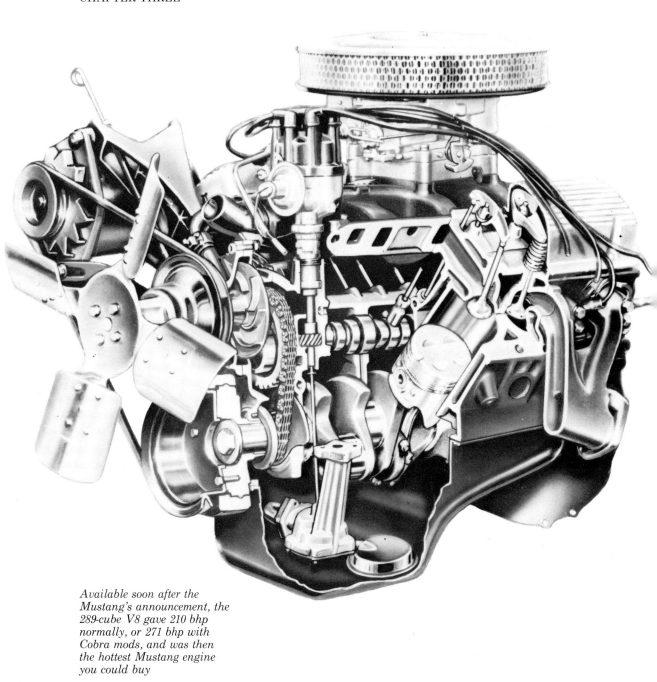

Available soon after the Mustang's announcement, the 289-cube V8 gave 210 bhp normally, or 271 bhp with Cobra mods, and was then the hottest Mustang engine you could buy

Falcon six-cylinder with three-speed, semi-synchro manual transmission, and these cars ran on 6.50 × 13 tyres. Interior trim was adequate without being luxurious, and instrumentation on the sparse side: just a band-type speedometer flanked by fuel and temperature gauges.

But the list of options seemed to go on for ever: even the screen washers, sun visors, back-up lights and exterior mirror were extras in those days of minimal equipment. The total of about fifty items included air-conditioning, power-assisted brakes and steering, a powered top for the convertible, push-button radio, a 'Rally-Pac' consisting of bolt-on tacho and clock, and various wheel-covers to simulate centre-lock hubs, wire wheels or whatever. A highly desirable Special Handling package at $38.60 included stiffer front springs and shocks, a thicker anti-sway bar, 14-inch wheels, and 16:1 (instead of 20:1) steering, giving $3\frac{1}{2}$ instead of $4\frac{1}{2}$ turns lock-to-lock. In the early days there was talk of an independent rear suspension layout derived from the Mustang I prototype. This, it was said, would be a feature of cars raced by Carroll Shelby and made available to a very limited number of private buyers— but it never happened.

The Mustang's V8 was the 260/164 (that's cubic inch/horsepower) Fairlane engine with two-barrel carburettor, known as the Challenger in Mustang circles. Almost immediately this was accompanied by a four-barrel 289/210 Challenger Special V8, it's output sometimes quoted as 225 rather than 210 bhp, and after a time this engine could be had in High Performance trim using goodies pioneered by Shelby's Cobra. With 10.5:1 compression ratio, solid lifters and dual exhausts (including twin manifolds or dual headers), it gave something like 271 bhp.

Basically there were four transmissions: the Six's three-speed manual box without first-gear synchro; a new all-synchro manual three-speeder for the two lower-powered V8s; Ford's Cruise-O-Matic three-speed auto transmission with manual restriction to the two upper ratios in snow or slush—this being offered with all but the hottest engine; and a four-speed, all-synchro manual box for the High-Performance engine which was also made available for the less powerful units. Axle ratios were normally 3.2 for Sixes in hardtop form, 3.5 for the heavier convertibles powered by the same engine, and an even 3.0 for V8s, with Ford's slightly unreliable limited-slip differential as a later option.

The early Mustang was greeted more enthusiastically by the public than by the press. I suspect that some writers had a genuine difficulty in deciding how the car should be judged, and they were not helped by the conflicting claims and comments that came from Dearborn. One Ford press handout claimed 'speed with safety up to 145 mph', although Iacocca himself was quoted as seeing the Mustang first as a family car, but in the words of *Car and Driver*, 'It's also aimed at a not-too-clearly-defined market consisting of customers looking for a not-too-well-defined combination of luxury and status. In addition to all this the Mustang is intended as a sports car (or sporty car).' Jack Prendergast, the executive engineer most closely associated with turning the Mustang concept into an actual automobile, was quoted by *Road & Track* as remarking that he didn't know whether he was building a family kind of sports car or a sports kind of family car, but 'whatever it's called, it's going to be something special in the way of driving fun.' *Motor Trend* seemed to be adopting a realistic viewpoint in saying that although the Mustang I prototype was 'a real sports car' the production Mustang was 'more like a nice-looking Falcon . . . Some will be disappointed by this Mustang, but we think most buyers will be more than satisfied with what it offers.' Which, of course, the sales figures amply confirmed, and it was a little unkind of *Road Test* to announce: 'The fastest-selling car in the world is a hoked-up Falcon with inadequate brakes, poor handling and marvellous promotion . . . Mustangs are poor road cars, no fun to drive,

Bucket seats and a floor shift were selling features of the original interior. The tachometer and clock on the steering column were part of the optional 'Rally-Pac'

and better than large cars only to the extent that they are less cumbersome.'

Road & Track subscribers had to wait for their May 1964 issue (published early April) because it was delayed to catch the Mustang release date, and six pages were devoted to the car. This, by Gene Booth, amounted to a hymn of praise: 'The Mustang is definitely a sports car, on par in most respects with such undisputed types as the MG-B, Triumph TR-4 or Sunbeam Alpine . . . The Mustang is not simply a special-bodied Falcon.' Booth praised the handling ('Seems to lift its nose and charge around the bends in easily controlled drifts . . . Body lean

Two views of the original hardtop model. The wheel-covers are an option known as 'simulated knock-off racing wheels'

is minimal . . . The spring rates provide admirable firmness'), and while admitting that the brakes were 'hardly on a par with any imported sports car', praised them nonetheless because 'Brake fade seemed less a problem than usual with domestic cars.'

It was a curious effort which seemed even more curious when, in the August issue of the same magazine, the staff writers reported on their experiences of driving three V8 models over some 2000 miles: 'The suspension was the same on all three cars we drove, as were the brakes, and it is difficult to find anything to say about either except that they were typical of the sedans Detroit

The original, deep-dished steering wheel called for a set-back driving seat, but rear passenger space (overleaf) was generous by European standards

has been producing. The ride is wallowy, there's a tendency for the car to float when being driven at touring speeds, and the 'porpoise' factor is high on an undulating surface . . . There seems little excuse for such frankly sloppy suspension on any car with the sporting characteristics which have been claimed for the Mustang.' *Road & Track* did approve of some features: 'We don't want to give the impression that we didn't like the Mustang. On the credit side is the appearance. It's an interesting, exciting car to look at . . . not simply gimmicked-up for the sake of attracting attention. The cost of the car is also to be appreciated. Even the completely loaded street version delivers at less than $3500 and this, compared with the near $5000 it takes to deliver a similarly equipped Sting Ray, makes it a bargain. The advantages of a full 4-seater cannot be overlooked either.

'We were disappointed, though, because the Mustang was so little different (except in appearance) from the typical American sedan. It seemed to us that Ford designers had a chance with the Mustang to genuinely improve the breed and introduce untold numbers of American drivers to driving pleasures they've never before experienced. Instead, they simply built all the familiar characteristics for which the typical American sedan has been cursed so long, into a sporty looking package.'

A month later, *Road & Track* came back yet again to the Mustang after testing one of the High Performance cars which were about to be marketed; it was a 289/271 V8 with four-speed transmission and full handling package, including 5.90 × 15 Firestone Super Sports tyres. 'A vast improvement in most respects over the previous models, and it is our opinion that the Mustang would be a better car if FoMoCo had made these suspension options standard equipment and progressed from that point. . . . The effect is to eliminate the wallow we experienced with previous Mustangs and to tie the car to the road much more firmly, so that in a fast

turn the point of one's departure to the boondocks is
delayed very considerably.' The weight distribution and
brakes remained a problem, it was thought: 'The high-
performance Mustang has 56% of its weight on the front
end, so that at very high speeds one has the feeling that
the front end will continue in the direction in which it is
pointing despite anything one does with the steering
wheel. But here, again, the suspension options improve
the actual situation considerably. . . . Our test car was
one of three prototype high-performance versions of the
Mustang, and we have been told that independent rear

suspension and disc brakes are to be included in the near future. These two items will add enormously to the car's virtues, and in particular the disc brakes, because the brakes on the standard versions were barely adequate and the additional speed of the high-performance car makes them quite inadequate.'

Car Life also preferred the HP version 'because of its obvious superiority to the more mundane everyday Mustang. Where the latter has a style and a flair of design that promises a road-hugging sort of performance and then falls slightly short of this self-established goal, the HP Mustang backs up its looks in spades. . . . The result is a fine-handling car capable of sticking to any highway at any speed it can attain . . . We can only add that this is the sort of Mustang that Ford ought to build more of; it has the guts of its namesake, the looks of a thoroughbred and the fleetness of a Native Dancer. It's been some time since we enjoyed a road test so much.' Both magazines quoted identical performance figures: a maximum of 120 mph at 6500 rpm, acceleration to 60 mph in 8.3 sec, and 15.9 for the standing quarter with a terminal 85 mph. Testing a similar car for *Popular Science*, Dan Gurney achieved 123 mph, 7.1 sec, 15.6 sec and 90 mph, which beat a 327/300 Corvette in all but top speed. Shelby's partner in All-American Racers said flatly: 'This car will run the rubber off a Triumph or an MG. It has the feel of a 2+2 Ferrari. So what *is* a sports car?'

In the homeland of the Triumph and MG, a High Performance Mustang supplied by Lincoln Cars of Brentford, London, was enthusiastically received for test by *Autocar* and *Motor*, although it was noted sadly that the tax-paid price in England was just under £2500. 'For those who want a car of outstanding performance,' said *Autocar*, 'the Mustang is one which is certainly different.' 'One of the most impressive performers we have tested,' said *Motor*, 'with tremendous acceleration available in all gears throughout a range from less than 1000 rpm to over 7000 rpm.'

*The first Mustang fastback,
also called the GT 2 + 2,
was an immediate success
when announced in
September 1964*

*From the side, the early
fastback revealed clean lines
and a good shape*

Both of the British magazines encountered a short-coming that had gone unremarked by their transatlantic contemporaries. *Autocar*: 'It was very pleasant to have an American car which handled as well as the Mustang—in the dry. . . . Unfortunately the Mustang, like most horses, hated wet weather. The back wheels seemed to lose all sense of adhesion and spend a good deal of their time trying to get ahead of the front ones. One has to drive the car with a feather-light foot in such conditions.' *Motor*: 'A basic understeer soon turned to power oversteer without actually losing adhesion, although this too was easy enough: once one gets accustomed to treading on the throttle with a sensitive toe, the handling is good . . . In the wet it is not a pleasant car to drive, as wheelspin is possible in all gears; corners

From the rear, the original fastback's lines were not so well balanced

must be taken with a maximum of discretion.' As to the brakes, *Autocar* found that 'the drum brakes used at present are almost worthless . . . Four stops made in quick succession from 80 mph faded the brakes so badly that the fifth stop took dangerously long.' And *Motor*'s view was: 'Fortunately disc brakes are an option. . . . The standard drum brakes on our test car were quite inadequate . . . Three laps of a four-corner circuit faded them to nothing, and it was possible to do this on a twisty country road using full acceleration between corners.'

The test car, ETW 566B, had either loosened up or been tidied up between the two magazines' tests, judging by the performance figures. *Autocar* recorded a two-way mean maximum of 115.7 mph, standstill to 60 mph in 8.2 sec and to 100 mph in 21.6 sec, and exactly 16.0 sec for the

Tested by Car Life *early in 1965, this hardtop had disc front brakes and the 289-cube engine which replaced the 260/164 Fairlane unit as the basic V8. It also had sidescoops without decoration, as on the then-new fastback. The plane is, of course, a Mustang fighter*

standing quarter. A few weeks later, *Motor* made the top speed 127.6 mph, with 7.6 sec to 60 mph, 19.7 sec to 100 mph, and 15.2 sec for the standing quarter.

September 1964 brought few changes in the hardtop and convertible models, but at last disc front brakes but not a servo were added to the options. The 170/101 engine—'a piece of machinery about as exciting as a dish of babyfood', in the opinion of *Car and Driver*—was replaced by a 200/120 six-cylinder, and the 260/164 V8 by a two-barrel 289/200. New to the line-up was a Mustang 2+2, intended for earlier production but delayed by tooling problems, and its looks were generally approved—indeed, some early buyers traded in their still-almost-new hardtops or convertibles to get one. 'It has a long, sleek profile and very harmonious proportions,' said *Car and Driver*. 'The air extractor louvres behind the side windows may not be a high point of styling, but at least they're functional, with air flow controlled by sliding buttons on the inside walls. . . . The interior is a fairly successful compromise between the need for a full rear seat and a sloping roof line. . . . In a manner reminiscent of the Barracuda, the rear seat folds forwards and leaves a spacious luggage platform. . . . The new fastback Mustang fitted with the 'handling package', disc brakes on the front wheels, and the high-performance version of the 289 V-8 is more closely comparable to a full-house Corvette than anything else in the Ford stable.'

Said *US Auto Sports*: 'The styling—although definitely short of truly great—has wide appeal. . . . The reaction of innocent bystanders is electric. You drive past a group of kids and they yell 'Mustang, Mustang.' It's weird. I can drive one of my Ferraris down the street and no-one looks up.' But the magazine's reporter, Ken Hutchinson, revealed that even in the USA some Mustang enthusiasts had found out about the rain: 'We felt that driving a Mustang in the wet is a good way to get hurt. . . . In those few moments after it begins to rain, we all but recommend parking it. We're not alone in our opinion. Ford threw a dinner and drinks for eighteen Mustang owners in the Chicago area . . . Nearly every one of the guests mentioned that they did not like the way it handled in the rain. Some had sixes, some 260s, some 289s, tires varied widely in size and manufacture, but it was agreed that regardless of how these options went together the car is deadly in the wet. Two of the eighteen had already crashed.'

Such criticism may have influenced Ford to put the tyre size of the Six up to 6.95 × 14 for 1966 while making a few small cosmetic changes: three horizontal chrome bars to each of the sidescoops; fancied-up wheel covers but a simplified front grille in which the Mustang mascot was allowed to 'float' without the doubtful benefit of vertical and horizontal chrome bars around it. Just in case anyone seized on this as an easy recognition feature, the front of the 2+2 was unchanged, with its two auxiliary lights and horizontal but no vertical bars, and this and the 'GT Package' models had no ornament at all on the simulated sidescoops. Inside, the five-gauge GT instrument layout was standardized for all models. With the 289/271 solid-lifter High Performance engine, now referred to as the Cobra V8, the Cruise-O-Matic transmission line was made available as an option.

In the April 1965 issue of *Car Life,* the early story of the Mustang was reviewed in a confusion of equine metaphors that must have been hard to sustain for three pages: 'It has been almost a year since the first of the thundering herd pounded over the horizon . . . There were those of us who detected the bloodlines of a thoroughbred, the sinewy stock of the tough cactusland cayuse and the nimble balance of a polo pony all blending in this hybrid breed. Those who saw this apparently numbered thousands and so began some of the most spirited horse trading ever seen inside this country's horse barns. During that year, Mustangs have been bought and branded in such ever-increasing numbers that only three other breeds can claim more action. . . . Few could perceive that man possessed

A British-registered fastback, photographed in 1966, has turn signals mounted beside the parking lights. The 1966 convertible and hardtop had no bars in the front grille and no auxiliary lights

another instinct, that American motorists, like their English cousins, could transfer affection towards a responsive and virile beast of steel, glass and rubber just as they had once done toward faithful hound and familiar horse.... We find ourselves growing attached to the Mustang. Those feelings it awakened in us when it first appeared have stayed with us and, if anything,

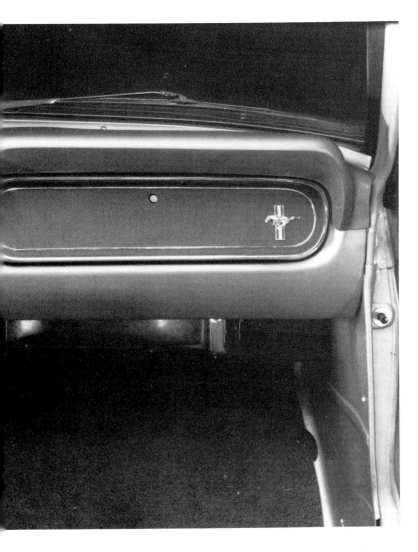

Part of the 'GT Package' before late 1965, this became the stock instrument set-up for 1966 Mustangs. A circular insert in the brake pedal shows the optional front discs are fitted, and the transmission is the Cruise-O-Matic type

intensified as we have saddled up successive specimens of the breed . . . To our way of thinking, it's right nice to see so many other folks riding and enjoying theirs, every time we ride into town or gallop through the countryside.'

Guess that's tellin' it just like it wuz, pardner.

'Stang '67/'68

Those who say the 1967 Mustang was designed to combat the Camaro are forgetting that the auto industry's idea of a reasonable gestation period makes a female hippo seem hasty: the 1967 Mustang was pretty well finalized before the end of 1964, when the Camaro project was still a closely guarded secret even inside General Motors. Tom Feaheny, the Ford engineer mainly responsible for the new version of the Mustang, put the record straight when he told Gary Witzenburg: 'The first Mustang had surprised a lot of people . . . with its success . . . Frankly, the amount of engineering effort in that car was not as great as it could have been . . . By mid-'64 we had a car that was a sensation in the marketplace, but we were getting criticized for some of its weaker aspects. We really wanted to do the job right the second time around.'

So far as styling was concerned, it was wisely decided that the Mustang must retain its distinctive identity, though the fastback was reshaped to link it more closely to Ford's increasingly successful sports/racer, the GT40. The pressing need to improve Mustang handling was recognized, and there were some new Falcon and Fairlane chassis bits that could be used to this end. But Ford's policy-makers had decreed that the reworked Mustang must also accept the big-block 390-cube engine, a considerable lump of iron that had been installed in everything from T-birds to trucks, not to mention (in its 427 cu. in. form) some of the hottest dragsters. This meant the unfortunate engineers not only had to sort out handling faults which they knew were mainly due to the

Mustang's nose-heaviness; they had to try and make sure they remained sorted when it was even *more* nose-heavy than before. Not easy. To quote Feaheny again: 'Given the primitive hardware of the day, I think the '67 Mustang was a really fine-handling car—more than just cornering ability, but a feeling of real security for the driver . . . I think all of us would have preferred to stay with the 289 engine rather than going to a 390, but it turned out to be a very acceptable package and handled quite well.'

On the racetracks, Ford were doing a fine job of reinforcing the company's new high-performance image. Jim Clark's 1965 Indianapolis win with the Lotus-Ford was followed in 1966 by the GT40's sweeping 1-2-3 at Le Mans, and the two race trophies Dearborn had most

For 1967, Ford produced a new and better-looking fastback Mustang with roofline carried all the way to the tail panel

59

coveted were safely on the sideboard. In September 1966, twelve days after the Shelby Mustangs of Yeager/Johnson, McComb/Brooker and Jerry Titus had won their category in the first Trans-Am sedan racing championship, Ford dealers were able to present the new Mustang range.

With the same 108 in. wheelbase, the track had increased considerably to 58 in., front and rear, and this was reflected in a width increase of more than two-and-a-half inches. The car was also two inches longer than before and a fraction higher (half-an-inch for the hardtop and convertible, a little more to improve headroom in the fastback), and the fuel tank held an extra gallon. At the front the grille was larger and the horizontal chrome bar had reappeared. The sides were subtly reshaped to improve the appearance of the sidescoops, and the main tail-panel was made concave. In the case of the 2+2 the reskinning of the body was more extensive, sweeping the roof-line out to the tail of the car to make a proper fastback out of a design that had previously hovered a little uncertainly between that and a notchback; it was a vast improvement on the original shape.

Inside, the seats and the instrument panel were remodelled, with a round speedometer and matching ammeter/oil pressure gauges, and three smaller gauges which were normally for fuel, coolant temperature and a clock (oddly enough, those who specified a tachometer lost the ammeter and oil pressure gauge!).

Tyre size for the six-cylinder cars was standardized at 695 × 14, and 'wide-oval' (i.e. low-profile) tyres could be had on the V8s. The lower arm of the front suspension linkage was lengthened by 2.5 in., the pivot point of the A-bracket was lower down, and there was a cam adjustment instead of shims to set camber and castor angle. With lower-friction steering joints, the manual steering ratio was changed to a quicker 25.3:1 and the power steering to an even better 20.3:1. There were now two optional suspension set-ups: the 'special handling package' offered stiffer springs and shocks and front

Longer and wider, the new fastback had a larger front grille, in common with the other 1967 models

anti-sway bar; the 'competition handling package' provided even stiffer springs, adjustable Koni shocks, an even heftier anti-sway bar, 16:1 ratio steering and 670 × 15 Super Sports tyres on six-inch rims, at a total extra cost of $388.53.

The brakes were still 9 in. drums for the Sixes and 10 in. for the V8s, but with the option of now power-assisted Kelsey-Hayes ventilated-disc front brakes as used on the Lincoln Continental and Thunderbird. There was a dual hydraulic circuit with rear-wheel pressure limiting valve, and several other new safety-inspired features which were becoming common to all cars.

Except for the addition of the 390/320 V8, the engine line-up was unchanged. With three transmission options—all-synchro three-speed or four-speed manual, plus Cruise-O-Matic—there were thirteen possibilities: the four-speed was not available with the Six, and the three-speed was not available with the 289/271 V8. There was a part-fancy, part-functional option of a GT Equipment Group that offered, with either of the hottest V8s, power-assisted discs, 'special handling' suspension, F70-14 wide-oval whitewalls, dual exhausts, auxiliary lamps in the grille, sidestripes and a louvred hood (bonnet) with turn signal telltales incorporated in it. Besides these there were, as usual, enough additional options to keep Mustang enthusiasts arguing forever about what is or is not a factory-supplied item. They included a set of safety-harness straps that made it impossible to reach either the handbrake or the wiper switch.

This time the press reaction was a whole lot different. Mario Andretti tried two '67 models for *Popular Science*, one 390 with and one without the GT equipment, and ended up with the comment: 'They've kept the best things from the old Mustang styling and cleaned up the details that were wrong. I think Ford has a winner here. It's definitely more car than the old Mustang—and I think it's more car than the Camaro, too.' *Car and Driver* said: 'Anyone who likes the old Mustang ought to go

The convertible and hardtop Mustangs were also reskinned for 1967, and had the same redesigned sidescoops in the rear fenders

63

Another change for 1967: separate tail light lenses

nuts for the '67,' and their opinion of the 390-cube engine was: 'In a heavy, full-sized Ford it ain't much to sound off about, but in a 3400-lb compact it comes on like spit on a griddle.' *Car Life* expressed slightly qualified approval of the 390, noting 'a tendency for the rear end of the automobile to hop about unduly,' but giving special mention to 'the remarkable ability of the car to stop quickly, surely and without loss of directional stability,' and the fact that with wide-oval Super Sports, 'bends were taken at high speed, but with a sense of security and a feeling of precise control that tires of lesser sticking quality do not provide.' And *Road Test*, which had condemned the Mustang quite mercilessly the first time around, said: 'The GT version comes off as a pretty keen car . . . This machine is a far cry from the Mustang we tested in our December 1964 issue, and we feel Ford is to be commended for improving the breed.'

Road & Track, which was getting to the stage of

*Mick Webber, of the Classic
American Auto Club in
Britain, owns this 1966
Mustang Six hardtop with
two-tone colour scheme*

Above left *Bertone's handsome
version of the Mustang, with
an appropriate New York
City background (Courtesy of*
Automobile Quarterly*)*

Above *David Barraclough
races his well-preserved
Shelby GT350 at Donington
in 1982*

Left *An example of the early
Shelby GT350 Mustang,
photographed in the USA by
Stanley Rosenthal*

8-15-69
S-14560-9

Above *Seen at the 1967
Chicago Auto Show,
Mustang Mach 2 was a mid-
engined two-seater and
actually used the 289-cube
engine, but it never went into
production*

Above right *One of the
earliest Mustang
advertisements, this is taken
from the 24 May 1964 issue of
New York Times*

Right *There was plenty of
punch in this 1967 Mustang
advertisement*

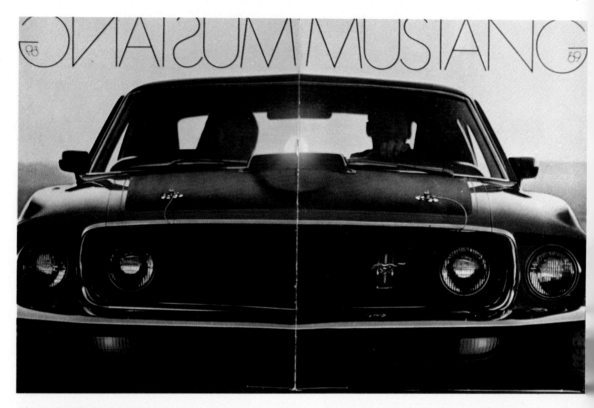

Above *The Mach 1 Mustang,
new for 1969, made an
appropriate cover for the 1969
Mustang catalogue*

Right *John Ewer's racing
Mustang at Snetterton, 1968,
for the 500-kilometres Guards
Trophy event*

Right *One of many special Mustangs built for Bob Tasca, president of Tasca Ford in Providence, Rhode Island, was this handsome version of the Boss 429*

Below *The new Grandé, introduced for 1969, was an up-market version of the Mustang 'SportsRoof'*

Mustang Grandé
your first Mustang
made life more delicious, right
So how about a second helping

Sheer luxury. All planned to reflect your lavish mood. As you can see from its very handsome styling and attractive appointments, such as wire-style wheel covers, dual racing-style mirrors and neat two-tone narrow tape stripes, Grandé says here is the elegant Mustang.
The standard 200-cubic-inch, 7-main-bearing Six is a lean-muscled, smooth performer. For greater punch, choose the larger, brand-new, 4.1 Litre six-cylinder engine. Provides added go with traditional Six economy. More power? Pick the spirited 302-cubic-inch V-8. Or one of five other V-8's all the way up to 335 hp.
Go with the standard 3-speed manual shift, or specify the two-way transmission: SelectShift. It'll do the shifting automatically, or you can go through the gears manually. You can downshift to low or second gear for manual control on hills, or for the fun of going through the gears. Comes with a sporty floor-mounted T-bar shift lever. Add a vinyl roof that looks like real leather — in either black or parchment. Nice touches outside. Now see what's in store for you inside— just turn the page.

liking any car so long as it was a Ferrari, dismissed the new Mustangs in a half-a-dozen lines. But *Cars* chose the Mustang as Top Performance Car of the Year for 1967. 'The 390 Mustang accelerates, handles, stops and looks like a "total performance" vehicle. It has everything going for itself in every respect. The hot-rodder can really appreciate the 390 Mustang because of all the 390 and 427 factory and California bolt-on, bolt-in and build-up goodies that are available. The sports car buff has the Cobra 271-hp route complete with Competition suspension to travel. And last, but not least, the average motorist has his or her choice of a myriad of dress-up, power, economy and convenience options to choose from when buying time rolls around. There's something for everyone.'

The base '67 Mustang carried a $2461.46 pricetag, but *Cars* hung so many extras on a 390 GT fastback that the actual price was nearer $4500. The magazine rated the extra cost well worthwhile. 'The new Mustang is one helluva machine—especially if you order it with the

Jackie Oliver, seen here at Silverstone in 1967, was one of the most prominent Mustang racers in Britain

Right *Well wound up at Brands Hatch, the Mustang dives through Bottom Bend*

Below *Another Silverstone picture shows Jackie Oliver's car in the Touring Car Championship of 1967*

Opposite page *For 1968, the treatment of the sidescoop changed yet again, being very restrained on the hardtop Mustang, but given an 'accent stripe' on the fastback*

right options. . . . From an appearance standpoint alone, our test Mustang comes on like an expensive imported Gran Turismo. From its sunken egg-crate-styled grille adorned with high-speed road lamps to its chevron-blinkered, quad-exhausted rear, the GT Mustang is all class.' The 390 was preferred because: 'The 271-hp 289 is a rough-idling, high-revving small-cuber which adds over $325 to the base price of a Mustang. The big brawny 390 puts out more horsepower, requires less maintenance and totals out to just $260 extra. . . . On the road it's very easy to take the big-cube 390 power. The car just doesn't feel like a Mustang. It feels much heavier and more substantial. . . . Considering the extra weight planted on the front end . . . the car is, in our opinion, an excellent handling compromise street machine. True, the car does understeer, but it's controllable.'

In its March 1967 issue, *Road & Track* ventured out of the pasta parlour long enough to compare the Mustang with its main rivals in the domestic market, the Barracuda and the Camaro. The conclusion was: 'Each of them is basically a compact sedan with a stylish body, with all the virtues and vices of the typical American sedan. True, each can be ordered with things like improved steering, braking, handling, instrumentation, etc. But in each case these things aren't a fundamental part of the concept. None of them offers anywhere near the best present-day standards in braking and handling. Each of them is built as a very plain car in standard form, and the options necessary to bring them up to the relatively simple form in which we tested them make them fairly expensive cars.

'On the other hand they all offer that one quantity at which American car builders are so capable—reliability. They are based on time-tested components and can be expected to last a long time with minimum service attention. Of the three, the Mustang was best liked by the staff. We feel that, if nothing else, the Mustang has demonstrated to the American public what a quality "small" car is. . . . Of the three, only the Mustang comes

Mustang publicity never got very far from the horse theme, and here the 1968 hardtop is seen in a corral-type setting. The side marker lights, front and back, are part of the Nader-inspired 'safety' package which also changed the interior design considerably

trimmed in standard form in such a manner as most buyers will want it; the other two must be optioned to the hilt or they look like rental cars.'

In terms of sales it was an excellent year for Ford, nicely rounded off by another Trans-Am category win for Mustang, and it came as no surprise that the Mustang was changed hardly at all for 1968. At the front, the horizontal grille bars gave way to a chrome ring, and the optional louvred bonnet with telltales was standardized for all models. The sidescoop decoration was altered for the umpteenth time, and the fuel filler cap changed again. Inside, Nader-inspired safety regulations called for a collapsible steering column which was given a new steering wheel, there was additional padding, and most of the handles, levers and controls were altered. The same regulations brought side marker lights, white on the front fenders and amber on the rear ones.

On the mechanical side, there were some changes to the optional disc brakes, and the front suspension incorporated a curved lower arm which reduced steering kickback. The biggest news concerned the engine line-up, for two had been dropped but there were three newcomers. The discontinued units were the higher-powered 289 V8s. The new engines were a four-barrel 302/230 V8, the same unit in 302/345 High Performance form, and a four-barrel 427/390, the hottest engine yet offered to the public for Mustang use. Presumably because of emission control equipment, the 200-cube six-cylinder was now rated at 115 instead of 120 bhp, the 289/200 at 195 bhp, and the 390/335 Thunderbird Special at 325 bhp.

Motor Trend did a careful, well-reasoned survey of the '68 Mustangs in its January 1968 issue, and still plumped for the 390-cube engine: 'We prefer the 390 GT V-8 for performance tasks, mostly because it's doubtful the average user would ever realize full potential from the 427, and probably be frustrated with the 302 4-bbl V-8. Getting full potential from a 427 dictates serious efforts on a closed course. . . . The performance-minded 390 GT

The 1968 models were offered with a new 302-cube engine, which gave 230 or 345 bhp depending on state of tune. This is the hotter one, with tunnel-port heads

V-8 is good for anywhere from 11 to 15 mpg, and 16 might be squeezed from it on a long trip. This isn't bad for an engine with almost constant power reserve . . . It's extremely mild mannered around town and doesn't act up in traffic or when the temperature climbs.' It was reckoned that 'The Mustang ride has been improved every year since its introduction, and this is the best yet . . . "Plain Jane" Mustangs without heavy-duty suspension feel good for '68, and offer about what buyers could expect from "handling packages" as far back as five years ago. Ford engineers have evidently become aware of the fact that there's more value in control than in a cushiony ride . . . ' The mpg figures quoted were of course for the smaller American gallon. From an Imperial gallon, an extra 20 per cent could be expected.

There are those who see 1968 as the ultimate year of the Mustang: good handling, a good range of engines, and dimensions that did not push it out of the compact category. But that would exclude the Mustang musclecars—Cobra Jet Ram-Air, Mach I, Boss 302 and Boss 429—which belong to the Bunkie Knudsen era. On February 6, 1968, just before the Chevrolet Camaros shamed the Mustangs at Sebring and paved the way for their production Z-28, Henry Ford II made headline news by hiring GM's toughest operator to become FoMoCo president. From then on, everybody started playing bears instead of ponycars, and the Battle of the Cubic Inches had begun in earnest.

'Stang '69/'70

In September 1968, Knudsen added spice to the launching of the 1969 Mustang range by sending Mickey Thompson to Utah with a 427 and two 302-cube Mach I models and three drivers, one rejoicing in the name of Bot Ottum. USAC regulations limited the engine modifications somewhat, it was said, but they had 14-quart sumps and twin oil-coolers, 37-gallon fuel tanks, truck axles with hefty torque arms, and asymmetric suspension to suit a 10-mile oval course laid out on the Salt Flats. The two 302s averaged 157.663 mph for 24 hours, cutting up the surface so much that the 427 could run for only 500 miles, but between them they bagged

New for 1969, the Mach I has the redesigned front with forward-jutting, four-lamp grille. The car is wider and slightly lower than before, and its sides are sharply sculptured, with the imitation sidescoops located high up on the "SportsRoof" and Mach I

some 300 records. *Cars* later remarked that the Utah Mustangs 'can't even be considered relatives of the show-room model,' but it kept Madison Avenue happy.

Although the wheelbase remained 108 inches, the 1969 Mustangs looked very, very different as the result of what was arguably the finest styling job anyone had yet done to the car. The sharply-jutting four-lamp front had more than a touch of Buick Riviera about it, maybe, but that was no bad thing; some of us privately believed that *any* change to the original Mustang front—including running it into a wall—could only be an improvement. The body sides, too, were much sharper with their bold sculpturing which blended well with the high-set sidescoops of the fastback model, now called the 'SportsRoof', but the convertible and hardtop had rather unfortunate cheese-grater devices which seemed to be vents rather than scoops. The hardtop formed the basis of a new and more luxurious Mustang called the Grandé,

All the Mustangs lost their quarter vents for 1969, but the Mach I had pivoted rear windows. The car was almost four inches longer overall, and the windscreen was more sharply raked

with an inexplicable acute accent which made it neither French nor Spanish (and Ford surely cannot have wanted it to be Puerto Rican?). This featured a very handsome interior, an extra 55 lb of sound insulation, and in the words of *Motor Trend*, 'enough optional goodies to make a salesman light up like a $50 slot-machine payoff in Vegas.' The Sports Roof, too, had its *alter ego* in the adrenalin-stirring shape of the Mach I with its matt-painted 'shaker scoop' hood and NASCAR-style locking pins on cables, which to *Cars* magazine 'comes on like no other Mustang ever produced, including the overrated, overpriced Shelby scoopmobile. It's just out of sight.'

In the process of restyling, Ford had made the Mustang almost four inches longer than its predecessor, adding all of this forward of the screen, which was now more steeply raked. The seating position was lower and the overall height slightly reduced, with almost half-an-

The new Grandé of 1969 had different rear fender scoops whose shape suggested a vent rather than an intake

Another view of the Grandé,
showing the side vents and
the modified tail

inch more width. By moving back the door-shut pillar some four inches, the door opening was made wider to improve access to the back seat, and rear leg-room was improved by moving one of the floor cross-members. Fuel tankage went up by three gallons, too. All models lost their quarter-vent windows, an economy also adopted by the other ponycar manufacturers, but the Mach I combined Porsche-like pivoting windows at the rear with Porsche-looking (but not Porsche-feeling) high-backed seats. Notable options included, for the first time, the much better Traction-Lok differential, and an exasperating three-spoke steering wheel that kept blowing the horn when you least expected it.

For 1969 the last of the 289-cube V8s was dropped, being replaced by an alternative 250/155 six-cylinder unexpectedly called the '4.1 Litre'—a touch of European

Not all testers liked the cornering behaviour of the Mach I, especially if it had the big 428-cube engine, like this car

snobbism, maybe. The 427/390 was also dropped after its short stint in the Mustang engine array, but there was a double duo of newcomers: a 351-cuber built at Windsor, Ontario, was rated at 250 bhp as a two-barrel and 290 with four-barrel carburettor; there were two four-barrel 428 cu in engines which seemed the same because both were quoted at 335 bhp, but were in fact very different. One was the hard-charging Cobra Jet Ram-Air job, whose real output Ford kept secret, probably to prevent Ralph Nader's disintegration in an outburst of righteous indignation. It was getting difficult to keep track of Dearborn's power plants. No wonder Paul van Valkenburgh of *Sports Car Graphic* once said: 'Call up Ford's Engine and Foundry to ask how many engine designs they've built recently and they'll say, "You mean right now, or by quitting time?"'

Interior of the Mach I was much less flashy than those of earlier models

*The Mach I 'shaker scoop'
protruded through a hole in
the bonnet*

The Mach I was available with any of the five bigger V8s, and the other models with any of the impressive eight-engine selection of two six-cylinders and six V8s, ranging from 200 to 428 cubic inches in displacement and from 115 bhp to at least three times that power output. The all-synchro manual three-speeder was standard wear with any but the 390 and 428 engines, and the Select-Shift Cruise-O-Matic, allowing manual hold on the two lower ratios, was an available option with any of the power plants. An all-synchro close-ratio manual box could be had with all but the two sixes and the smallest V8, and a wider-ratio box was optional with any V8 except the two 428s.

To accommodate the big 428 engines the track was made half-an-inch wider, front and rear, and Ford copied GM by putting staggered shocks at the rear, one ahead of and one behind the axle, in a not entirely successful effort to control tramp with the high-torque engines. Normal tyres were C78-14 with the three smallest engines, E70-14 wide-ovals on the 351-cube Mach I, and various others according to the engine chosen.

The Ford catalogue naturally invited customers to dress up their Mustang 'like it was built for Parnelli—one of the Jones boys,' and Uncle Tom McCahill said the '69 cars he tested for *Mechanix Illustrated* were 'loaded like Duck Mouth Finnegan at a brewery party.' Because of its appearance the Mach I got the lion's share of attention, but did it perform the way it looked? The magazines were divided in their opinion of the car, and whether it was better with 351 or optional 428 engine. To *Car Life*, the Mach I with 428 Cobra Jet was 'Best Mustang yet', but *Car and Driver*'s assessment of the same model was: 'It may just be that this time the stylists have done *too* good a job. Look at the Mustang Mach I and you expect miracles—drive it and they are not forthcoming.'

The dragster-style 'shaker scoop' protruded through a hole in the bonnet and, being fixed to the carburettor, waggled about in front of the driver as the engine rocked

Above *Driving along, the Mach I owner could watch the shaker scoop move*

Opposite top *The Boss 302 was a clever reshaping of the 1969 SportsRoof inspired by Knudsen. At his insistence, the fake scoops in the rear fenders were at last eliminated*

Right *The rear spoiler of the Boss 302 was adjustable, and the bonnet was normally painted matt black. Rear-window louvres were optional*

Biggest-engined of Mustangs was the Boss 429, described by designer Roy Lunn as 'just a hairy, crazy road machine'

on its mountings. It had a trap that opened to admit cold air for maximum acceleration, and experiments proved this was worth 0.2 sec on a standing quarter-mile—but good driving could make a difference of almost two seconds over the same distance. McCahill took 6.3 and 17.6 sec to reach 60 and 100 mph, with a 15.4-sec standing quarter. *Car Life* clocked only 5.5 sec, 12.8, and 13.90. *Car and Driver* did pretty well with 5.7, 14.3 and 14.3 sec, but despite this, commented: 'The test car has 2140 of its 3607 lbs balanced on the front wheels, and that's with a full gas tank. *Fifty nine point three* per cent of its weight . . . Any rear-wheel-drive car would be hamstrung with that kind of weight distribution, and the Mustang is no exception. It can't begin to put its power to the ground for acceleration.'

To *Car Life*, however: 'The Mach I goes like the hammers in a straight line.' On the subject of cornering: 'Constant readers are surely braced for the standard lecture about too much weight forward, with its attendant dreaded understeer. Relax. The lecture doesn't apply to the Mach I. The greatness shows up best on a winding mountain road. By choosing the optimum combination of suspension geometry, shock absorber valving and spring rates, Ford engineers have exempted the Mach I from the laws of momentum and inertia, up to unspeakable speeds.' Quite a trick, but *Car and Driver* encountered no such miracles: 'When it comes to handling, the most charitable thing to say is that the Mustang is all thumbs . . . Does it understeer? Yes sir, yes sir, three bags full . . . In really hard cornering situations, steering wheel corrections of a quarter-turn have virtually no effect on the direction of travel . . . For those really interested in handling, we'd suggest the smaller 351 cubic inch V-8.' *Canada Track and Traffic* felt the same: 'Forget the CJ motor . . . The Mach I with the CJ is not a well-rounded package . . . seems bent on a self-destruction. When we try to turn the corner, it wants to continue in a straight line. It becomes obvious very quickly that the Mach I's cornering ability doesn't

Left *Karl Ludvigsen's picture of the prototype Boss 429 was taken in January 1969, so the Ram-Air intake has understandably been blanked off*

Below *Based on the Boss 302, the Trans-Am racer used by Parnelli Jones looks almost tame compared to the 'street' Boss 429*

match its very considerable straight-line speed . . . We tried the Mach I with the 351 cu. in. engine and found an amazing difference in the handling. On Ford's tight-cornered "handling" test track, the Mach I with the 351 could run away from its huskier brother.'

Whether or not the 428 Cobra Jet Ram-Air version of the Mach I rates as a balanced high-performance vehicle, *Science and Mechanics* probably hit on the real reason for marketing such an ego-boosting automobile: 'For a very long time Ford Motor Company has been out to lunch on the street scene. It was no secret that the production Ford-built cars were not up to running with the red-hot machines that Chevy and Pontiac were turning out. Ford seemed to be more interested in winning image events like Le Mans than in winning sales in the youth market . . . So now they've done something about it.' Never mind the World Sports Car Manufacturers' Championship; the kids will be far more impressed if your Mustang sets light to its tyres—even if it's only because of faulty weight distribution.

Reshaped again for 1970, the Mustang had another new front with simulated air intakes where the previous year's outer lamps had been. This is the Grandé, showing that the sidescoops or vents disappeared under Knudsen's influence

The Mach I design, good or bad, was already settled when Bunkie Knudsen came on the scene from General Motors, and naturally he had a few ideas of his own. He told Larry Shinoda, a Japanese American he had brought with him from GM, to build a production Mustang that would beat GM's Camaro Z-28 in *every* way, and its name was a monosyllabic statement of its intended role—'Boss'. In appearance it was a simple but very effective reshaping of the 1969 SportsRoof without fake sidescoops, shaker-scooped and lock-pinned hood or any such gewgaws; only the louvred rear window suggested gimmickry, and that was an option. The track was half-an-inch wider, front and rear, and the front suspension anchorages had been strengthened considerably to cope with the big F60-15 Goodyear tyres on seven-inch-rimmed steel wheels. All around, the stock suspension was the equivalent of a handling package, and the steering was of 16:1 ratio with or without power assistance. Power-assisted disc brakes were also standard, there was a larger front spoiler or 'plow', and an

Except for its new front and a different paint job, the Boss 302 changed little in appearance for 1970

The Mach I still looked aggressive for 1970, but its cleaned-up front was spoiled by fake auxiliary lights which imitated the genuine lamps in the front grille of the 1968 Shelby Mustang

adjustable spoiler on the tail. The normal engine was a remodelled 302-cuber with new canted-valve heads, rated at 290 bhp with a four-barrel carburettor on a high-rise manifold but capable of being tuned to give more like 450 bhp.

Always a Mustang fan, *Car Life* took to the Boss 302 right away after comparing it with a Z-28, and reckoned: 'Had we been able to put the two cars on the strip at the same time, the Boss would have pulled the Z-28 off the line and held its lead until both cars were wound tight.

Then the Z-28 power would show and it would catch the Boss at the quarter-mile finish line. . . . On the street the Boss 302 is more flexible . . . easier to drive in a casual manner. . . . Wearing bigger tires puts the Boss ahead in terms of sheer cornering power. . . . We conclude with a victory for the Boss 302 . . . easier to drive slowly, and easier to drive fast.' This time, *Car and Driver* agreed: 'What the Shelbys should have been but weren't. . . . The best handling Ford to come out of Dearborn.' *Sports Car Graphic* also compared the Boss 302 with the Z-28, and, claiming: 'What is the difference? There ain't none!', they quoted identical acceleration times all the way, including 7.1 sec to 60 mph, 16.8 sec to 100, and 15.0 dead for the standing quarter.

A remarkable offshoot of the Boss 302 was the Boss 429, also produced (but by Roy Lunn instead of Matt Donner) in response to a Knudsen edict. For NASCAR racing, Ford needed to qualify their top-line hemi-head 429 engine which was used by drag and stock-car operators, and Knudsen decided to do it by building a run of 500 or more 429 versions of the Boss Mustang on a special assembly line. The 429 block being even wider than the 428, Lunn had to shift the front shock towers outwards, and the front track became 59.3 in., while the front end was lowered by an inch. Four-speed manual transmission was linked to a limited-slip (locker) axle, the springing was harsh and the front and rear anti-sway bars were enormous. The staggered rear-shock arrangement was used and power steering was standardized, as were non-servo front disc brakes.

As fitted in the Boss 429, the engine was potentially but not actually tremendous, being a curious mixture of good and bad. It had tough, forged pistons and rods with half-inch bolts, a high-nickel block and four bolts to each of the centre mains. The aluminium cylinder heads featured large ports, crescent combustion chambers and canted valves of considerable diameter. But instead of gaskets, the heads were fitted by means of 'dry decking'—separate O-rings for the combustion cham-

John Holman of Holman-Moody talks things over with Parnelli Jones at the Bridgehampton Trans-Am race of 1969

bers, water and oil passages. There was only one four-barrel carburettor on an engine that could have used two, and although it gave more than its rated 375 bhp, the Boss 429 was in fact never as fast as a well-turned-out Cobra Jet Ram-Air 428; it even had hydraulic lifters in 1969, although these were changed to solids for 1970. In the words of Wallace Wyss, writing in *Old Cars*: 'Suffice to say that in dead stock form the Boss 429 was a sleeping giant "out for the count". But if you merely installed headers, decent carburetion and a wilder cam, the giant woke up and began to look around. At 3000 rpm, with the mods, the giant suddenly begins to jump up and down and rip trees out alongside the road.' Let's hope he wasn't referring to the handling.

After success in the first two series of Trans-Am races the Mustangs had failed in 1968 and 1969, blowing their engines one year and—usually—their tyres the next. On September 3, 1969, Ford announced the new Mustang line-up for 1970. On September 7, Ronnie Bucknum's Camaro made sure that a Mustang could not win the Trans-Am. On September 11, Henry Ford II told Knudsen to go; it was assumed that the tough ex-GM executive had upset too many people in his year and a half at Dearborn. The most obvious change in the Mustang for 1970 was that the four-lamp front had been dropped after only a year, the outer lamps being replaced by simulated air-scoops in the front mudguards—but the scoops in the rear mudguards had disappeared, as on the Boss body. The Mustang motif had galloped back to its old place in the centre of the now wider grille, except on the Mach I, which had a fussy-looking front with imitation lamps set into it. Some of the sporty features which had appeared on the hotter cars in 1969 were now available with cooler machinery, either as stock items or as options. All had the high-back seats of the Mach I, and the Boss spoilers and rear window louvres could be had on any fastback model. All had fibreglass-belted tyres, and high-ratio manual steering was now an option; there were several steering wheels, all of oval shape. New

Transatlantic effort: George Follmer races a Boss 302 in the Trans-Am series at Bridgehampton and Frank Gardner races his similar Mustang in the Tourist Trophy race at Silverstone

'grabber' exterior colours and a wide choice of interior trims were part of the package. One of the new options was a seatback latch that released automatically when either front door was opened.

There were minor changes to the existing engines, plus an extensive revamp of the big-block 351, which had been completely redesigned when production moved from Windsor to Cleveland, with the aim of making it a likely contender for further development. The transmission systems were as before, but with a Hurst shifter on the manual four-speeders. For this, there was even an optional reverse lock-out to use in competition work.

Bob Kovacik of *Sports Car Graphics* liked the new engine a lot when he tried it in a 1970 Mach I: 'When Mach I was first introduced the performance engine was the 428, a heavy, brutish powerplant that detracted from the car's otherwise nimble characteristics. The new 351 Cleveland has reduced much of the front-end heft, and gives excellent acceleration as well.' As a dragster, though, the 351 Mach I certainly didn't measure up to the 428 Cobra Jet or even the Boss 302, judging by the magazine's quoted times: 8.3 sec to 60 mph, 20.2 to 100, and 16.1 sec for the standing quarter with a terminal speed of only 88.7 mph. The same magazine's Paul van Valkenburgh, by no means a Mustang fan, agreed rather grudgingly: 'I've got to admit the 351 Cleveland Mach I is pretty lively,' and also said: 'The handling is quite tolerable . . . With the power available, those (Goodyear) tires make breakaway and recovery as smooth and natural as driving a porch swing. A little noisy and a little smoky, perhaps, but that's show biz.'

It is on record that the first Mustang to appear in a road race was a 1964½ hardtop 260-cube V8 driven by Bill Clawson, a Ford engineer, at Waterford Hills, Michigan, and it is also on record that this car's brakes and handling were so excruciatingly bad that it was beaten easily by a tweaked Volkswagen Beetle. Ford had to learn a lot to score in the early Trans-Am races, and they learned a whole lot more to win the Trans-Am title back

*Interior decor of a Trans-Am
Mustang is strictly functional*

Under-bonnet view of a 1969 Trans-Am Mustang reveals two four-barrel Holley carburettors on high-rise manifolds

again in 1970, an achievement that made a good impression because it took more than a bottomless bank account to do it. *Road and Track* celebrated the occasion with a full road test of George Follmer's second-place Boss 302 (Parnelli Jones's winning car had gone on display around the showrooms). The magazine said simply: 'The Mustang did everything better than we expected. And our expectations were high. As anyone who's seen the 1970 Trans-Am cars will confirm, the Mustangs were the best cars in the series. They went faster and lasted longer than the others, within the same set of rules.

'To fully appreciate how good the Trans-Am Mustang is, you need two baselines, one for the production version of the car and another for the rules within which the street Mustang becomes a racing car. As it comes from the showroom, a 1970 Boss 302 Mustang weighs 3400 lb, divided 56 percent front, 44 percent rear. With the engine, suspension, brakes, wheels and tires included in the option, the car will do the standing quarter-mile in 14.8 sec, can hit 120 mph without engine damage, will stop from 80 mph in 300 ft and will corner at 0.73g. It is a good domestic performance car, competitive—but no more than that—with the others in class.

'The rules, nutshelled, let the builder do whatever he wants with whatever the factory chooses to sell. Minimum weight is 3200 lb, maximum engine size 5 liters or 305 cu in. . . . All Trans-Am cars are equipped with disc brakes fore and aft . . . Bud Moore says that the best of his engines develop 465 bhp with the average being 455 or 460. The engine in Follmer's car was average, he said. Since it was built, it had been through practice, qualifying, a race and a day-long thrashing for a television commercial. As it was, the quarter mile time (12.9 @ 110 mph) is good enough to impress a drag racer.

'Most of the work on the car involves the chassis and suspension . . . The racing Mustangs aren't stripped down. Ford sends the body/chassis structure and the various panels as they come before assembly. Moore's crew builds a roll cage—actually a space frame installed to stiffen the chassis as well as protect the driver—inside the hull, and mounts the various suspension pieces to that.

'The cornering characteristic is mild understeer, deliberately. Roll stiffness is adjusted with the front and rear anti-roll bars. There are racks of bars, in graduated sizes, carried on the van. Follmer and Jones can order whatever handling they want and the crew can supply it.'

Performance times were taken with George Follmer driving, and as the magazine pointed out: 'The car was not geared for standing starts and Follmer doesn't make them very often. . . . He shifted carefully, an intact transmission being more important than a split second in road racing. Each upshift was made at 7500 rpm, the engine's peak.' That being so, the acceleration times were excellent but not outstanding: 5.5 sec to 60 mph, 11.4 sec to 100. The quoted speeds in the gears were more impressive: first gear, 71 mph; second, 103; third, 124; fourth, 151 mph at 7500 rpm. And the fuel consumption? It was a terrifying 4 mpg.

After driving the car (whose weight distribution was 51/49), *Road and Track*'s tester noted that: 'An over-correction, especially entering a turn, will break all four wheels loose at once, and the car skips sideways. This happens more quickly than it can be told. . . . The suspension has been honed to a fine edge and there is no perceptible torque or roll steer. . . . It is our nature, maybe even our profession, to second guess and point out ways various people and companies could improve their products. For once, nothing. We don't know how one would build a better Trans-Am car.'

CHAPTER SIX

Cowboys

Checking back, I find the first piece I wrote about Carroll Shelby was published in *Autosport* in the mid-1950s. It may have been then that I first met the tall Texan, or later when I was 'ghosting' material for Roy Salvadori, the British racing driver who was one of the steadiest but certainly not one of the slowest men in the Aston Martin team. The two drivers had a good, relaxed relationship which made them a formidable pair in longer-distance races, and when Ol' Shel finally worked out which of the hotel dishes kept making him sick at Le Mans, he and Salvo pulled it off for Astons in 1959. Both had a wicked sense of humour, but I think it's fair to say they were two of nature's survivors—as team manager Reg Parnell learned when he confiscated as team trophies the expensive wristwatches they were given after the race. The two comedians reported him to the airport Customs officer on arrival in England, and he had to hand the watches over to avoid paying duty.

I wish I had known Shelby well enough to discover that we shared a deep affection for that wonderful man, Capt George Eyston. When I first attended the Sebring 12 Hours in 1965, Eyston and I had done a double act for the local MG Club the previous night at nearby Jacksonville, and had I checked out in the morning as early as he did—not an easy thing to do—the Mustang I tried at Sebring might have been one of the new GT-350 fastbacks instead of just an ordinary hardtop belonging to one of our photographers. Funny how an opportunity can pass you by.

Opposite top *Carroll Shelby—Texan Mustang trainer*

Opposite below *The original Shelby GT350 Mustang in 'street' form*

Shelby chucked racing during 1960 because of incipient heart trouble, and late the following year he got Dearborn interested in turning the long-established British A C sports car into the Shelby Cobra, powered by Ford's new small-block 260 and later 289-cube V8 engine, with results that are now part of motor racing history. So naturally Ford thought of Shelby when they wanted to jazz up the new Mustang for B-Production racing, and before the end of 1964 the Texan had a dozen race-prepared Mustangs ready to show them. With maximum effort from all concerned, there were 100 modified Mustangs ready for the S C C A to approve on January 1, 1965, and they were shown to the press some three weeks later. By that time they had a name: GT-350. Allegedly this was the distance in feet between two adjacent buildings at the Shelby plant in California, but that's probably a typical, tongue-in-cheek Shelby story. The

Another view of the GT350 in its typical Shelby colour scheme

289-cube engine normally gave a little over 300 bhp in tuned form, but not that much over.

In those days Shelby took in the chassis and panels from San Jose, reworked the suspension completely with altered front-end geometry and four-leaf springs at the rear plus Konis all round, and fitted torque arms to control the back axle. Goodyear 775-15 Blue Dots on six-inch rims were the normal tyre wear, the spare was placed behind the front seats and the battery moved to the trunk. Big Kelsey-Hayes disc brakes went on the front end, with 10-inch drums behind, and the steering drop-arm was lengthened to give quicker control. Transmission was by a close-ratio all-synchro manual Warner T-10 box, with a No-Spin truck locker axle. A flatter wood-rim steering wheel marginally improved the rather poor Mustang driving position, but the stock seats were retained and there were a couple of extra instruments, awkwardly placed in the middle of the dash.

The engine had a four-barrel Holley on a high-riser manifold, a 6½-quart sump and a revised exhaust terminating ahead of the back wheels. The bonnet was of fibreglass with central scoop and lockpins, and the radiator was enlarged. To Shelby the car was a Shelby, and the Mustang motif was either moved to one side of the grille or removed altogether. Racing versions were of course stripped out, with lightweight seats and plastic windows, more air scoops, a back axle oil-cooler, more fuel capacity and an interior roll-bar, but the weight distribution was little better and the cornering technique was a bit special. Except for this, *Road & Track* quite liked the car, recording 6.8 sec to 60 mph, 14.6 sec for the standing quarter and a maximum of 124 mph. But it was a rough and noisy $4311-worth, and first-year sales barely exceeded 500 cars. Something less than impressed by this, Dearborn called on Shelby to soften the car up for 1966. This was done (although the new Shelby options included a Paxton supercharger said to lift

The Shelby Mustang in track form: no bumpers, a deep cutaway for extra engine cooling, and brake-cooling ducts in the fibreglass front apron

engine power to 400 bhp), and sales almost trebled. In addition, 936 black-and-gold Shelbys were sold to Hertz, of all people, for their widely-publicized 'rent-a-racer' scheme. As the real racers had become known as the GT-350R, naturally the Hertz cars were GT-350H. They had auto-transmission, but would-be hirers had to be aged 25 or more, and were required to demonstrate that they could drive without bending the Shelby Mustang.

Ford took the softening-up process still further for 1967, when the fibreglass body parts (including a cowled grille and spoiler tail) were in fact Dearborn-designed. But the Shelby influence played an important part in the Trans-Am successes of 1966 and 1967, and the handsome new GT-500 powered by the 428-cube big-block engine made a good impression. Although the suspension mods had been simplified to save money, *Road & Track* found the handling surprisingly acceptable, but couldn't get within two seconds of the 13.5-sec standing quarter that Ford claimed for the car, and noted 'the highest fuel consumption of any street version car we've tested in

The early street Shelby had a woodtrimmed wheel, 8000 rpm tachometer and an oil pressure gauge

years.' They averaged 9.8 mpg. Without options, the GT-500 was listed at $4395.

For 1968, Shelby Mustang production was moved from California to Michigan and the Shelby touch pretty well disappeared altogether. Both cars were noticeably heavier and the GT-350 lost its hot 289 engine in favour of a much milder 302/250. Nevertheless, sales improved considerably, helped by a new convertible which at least *looked* good. When the Cobra Jet Ram-Air version of the 428-cuber became available during 1968, open or closed versions of the GT-500 with this power plant were dubbed GT-500KR. The initials stood for 'King of the Road', and nobody has recorded Joseph Lucas's re-action. The disappointments on the production side were matched by happenings on the track, where Shelby's Mustangs lost the Trans-Am title in 1968 and 1969, and when the title was regained in 1970 it was achieved by the rival Bud Moore Mustang team, not by Shelby.

The 1969 Shelby cars—if they could still be given that name—were built in another Michigan factory, and

The track Shelby had Plexiglass (Perspex) windows, and the rear-quarter vents were sealed by pop-riveted panels

113

were notable only for their profusion of wax-job scoops and stripes, except that the GT-350's engine changed again to the 351/290 Windsor unit. Production ended in November 1969, the last few hundred cars being tarted up further to make them 1970 models. It was sad, really, that corporate policy and economics—plus the ever-tightening stranglehold of emission laws—turned what had once been a promising if unsubtle automobile into an example of paintbrush engineering, which it was to

an even greater extent when revived for the Mustang II series under the name of Cobra.

There is some discrepancy in the figures quoted for total Shelby Mustang production in the 1965/1969 build period. In his painstakingly researched Mustang history Gary Witzenburg quotes 10,825, but this may omit the 1967 figure. Al Bochroch makes it 14,810, and it seems that no two sources agree on sub-totals for individual model years or types. For motoring historians, that's life.

Very different in appearance from the standard Mustang, the G T500 convertible of 1968 was designed and built by Ford, despite the 'Shelby' tag

Above *In 1969, the last year of the Shelby Mustangs, the closed versions of the GT350 and GT500 still looked good in side view, but the front end (top right) featured too many lamps and stripes and air intakes; there were even fender scoops at the front as well as the rear*

Right below *Originally a good looker, the GT500 convertible had also become rather gimmicky in appearance by 1969*

Barney Clark and Bob Cumberford commissioned Carrozzeria Intermeccanica to build this very businesslike Mustang station wagon

Commissioned by Scott Bailey, the Automobile Quarterly *Mustang was completed by Bertone in time for the New York Auto Show of 1965*

When a car attracts as much attention as the Mustang has done, there are always people who want to restate it in some way. Shelby designed an alternative production car, and at one time built it in quantities that Morgan, say, would rate stupendous. Others produced one-offs related visually or mechanically to the Mustang theme, to express an opinion of their own. One of the most handsome special Mustangs was the car that L. Scott Bailey of *Automobile Quarterly* commissioned Bertone to build on a 1964 chassis; it appeared at the 1965 New York Auto Show and was seen at various others before being sold by a dealer in Monte Carlo, but nobody seems to know where it is now. Another excellent vehicle was the Mustang station wagon which Barney Clark and

Bob Cumberford commissioned Intermeccanica to build out of a 1965 Mustang—which they did so well that one wishes it had become a production model. But a third attempt at an Italian Mustang, the OSI coupé seen at the 1965 Turin Show, was something else: on an all-independent short-wheelbase chassis with Mustang engine they had mounted what Henry Manney described as: 'A putty-colored fiberglass machine with a modified Testudo front, a Cobra coupé center section and a TVR backside.'

In England, Ken Rudd was converting Mustangs to right-hand-drive by the beginning of 1965, and in 1968 Ferguson Research demonstrated a four-wheel-drive Mustang to the motoring press, who didn't seem all that interested. In Australia, Pete Geohegan won the Touring Car Championship four times with two Mustangs which he had rebuilt himself, even to the extent of designing and making his own disc brakes. In the States, Gas Ronda was getting 10,000 rpm out of an sohc hemi 427 in 1966 to record elapsed times in the eights and a terminal velocity of more than 160 mph in something that might loosely be called a Mustang, having a fibreglass body of that shape hovering above a 112-inch wheelbase chassis. Ron Pellegrini and Johnny Malik produced a 'Super Mustang' for S/FX dragging, clocking 166 mph and more on nitro with their mildly-modified device which had a fibreglass Mustang body (16 inches shorter than standard) on top of a 96-inch wheelbase chassis, and a Dearborn-defying Chrysler 398-cube engine complete with supercharger. Mustang, indeed!

The students of Chaffey College in Southern California enjoyed themselves designing and building a Shelby-equipped Mustang with a 510 bhp, 351-cube Cleveland engine, in which Ak Miller took the Class C sedan record at a pretty impressive 172.837 mph, but even this pales into insignificance beside Connie Kalitta's Mustang Funny Car with 429 hemi engine, which in 1966 covered the standing quarter in 7.2 sec and recorded a terminal velocity of 221.12 mph.

Gas Ronda's Mustang dragster takes off in the NHRA Winter Nationals. By 1966 he was exceeding 160 mph with a highly-tweaked 427-cube engine running at 10,000 rpm

Another remarkable dragster loosely called a Mustang— though it had a supercharged Chrysler engine—was Ron Pellegrini's machine with tubular chassis and fibreglass body, capable of more than 166 mph on nitro fuel

My favourite, though it is not the fastest, is the whimsical creation of Tex Collins, the Hollywood stuntman known as 'Mr Cal Automotive'. He spent $50,000 installing a supercharged V12 Allison engine from a WW2 Mustang fighter plane—what else?—in a special chassis topped with a fibreglass replica of a 1970 Mustang car body, and braked by twin parachutes. The power output at 9.5 psi boost was reckoned to be something like 3500 bhp, definitely an advance on the Secretary Six. Admittedly his time for the standing quarter was no better than Kalitta's at 7.2 sec and his terminal velocity was far below, at a mere 204 mph. But what other Mustang in all the world had 28 litres displacement (1710 cubic inches)? And twenty-four exhaust pipes?

Ak Miller's long-snout Mustang, built by students at Chaffey College in Southern California, took the Class C sedan record at Utah with a speed of just over 172 mph

Brochure specifications

1965/66

BODY TYPES Hardtop and Convertible (plus Fastback from September 1964)

DIMENSIONS Wheelbase = 108 in. (2743 mm); Front track = 55.4 in. (1407 mm) on Sixes, 56.0 in. (1422 mm) on V8s; Rear track = 56.0 in. (1422 mm); Length = 181.6 in. (4613 mm); Width = 68.2 in. (1732 mm); Height = 51.1 in. (1298 mm); Luggage space (Hardtop) = 9 cu. ft (254.7 litres); (Convertible) = 7.7 cu. ft (218 litres) with top down; (Fastback) = 5 cu. ft (141.5 litres), or 18.5 cu. ft (523.6 litres) with rear seat folded; Approx weight (Hardtop) = 2562 lb (1163 kg); (Convertible) = 2740 lb (1244 kg); (Fastback) = 2621 lb (1190 kg); Fuel capacity = 16 US gal. (13.33 Imp. gal., 60.56 litres)

COLOUR AND TRIM Choice of 16 body colours and 5 all-vinyl trims (16 for 1966)

SUSPENSION Front, coil spring to upper A-bracket; Rear, 4-leaf semi-elliptic springs, diagonally-mounted shock-absorbers

STEERING Recirculating ball, ratio 27:1 (manual) or 22:1 (power-assisted)

BRAKES Drum front and rear, dia = 9 in. (228.6 mm) on Sixes, 10 in. (254 mm) on V8s. Option of front disc brakes for 1966.

TYRES Rayon cord, 4-ply, 6.50 × 13 on Sixes for 1965, 6.95 × 14 on V8s for 1965 and on all models for 1966

ENGINES 200 cu. in. (3.86 in. × 3.13 in.) Six (3277 cc, 98.04 mm × 79.5 mm), with 9.5:1 compression ratio, single-barrel carburettor and hydraulic valve lifters, rated at 120 bhp. Option of:

289 cu. in. (4.00 in. × 2.87 in.) V8 (4736 cc, 101.6 mm × 72.9 mm), with 9.3:1 compression ratio, 2-barrel carburettor and hydraulic valve lifters, rated at 200 bhp, or;

289 cu. in. V8 with 10.0:1 compression ratio, 4-barrel carburettor and hydraulic valve lifters, rated at 225 bhp, or;

289 cu. in. V8 with 10.5:1 compression ratio, 4-barrel carburettor, solid valve lifters and dual exhaust, rated at 271 bhp

TRANSMISSIONS 3-speed manual with synchromesh on second and top; Synchro-Smooth (3-speed all-synchro manual); 4-speed, all-synchro close-ratio manual; Cruise-O-Matic (3-speed auto with 3-speed range for normal driving, or 2-speed starting in second for slippery conditions, sequence P-R-N-Drive-L).
With 200/120 Six, 3-speed part-synchro transmission is standard. With 289/200 or 289/225 V8s, 3-speed all-synchro transmission is standard. With 289/271 V8, 4-speed close-ratio manual transmission is standard. Cruise-O-Matic optional with all engines (except for 289/271 in 1965). Four-speed manual optional with all engines
GENERAL Fully-aluminized exhaust system. 12-volt electrical system with 45 amp-hr battery. Full-flow oil filter (6000 miles, 10,000 km). Dry-element air cleaner (36,000 miles, 60,000 km)

1967

DIMENSIONS Wheelbase = 108 in. (2743 mm); Track front and rear = 58.0 in. (1473 mm); Length = 183.6 in. (4663 mm); Width = 70.9 in. (1801 mm); Height (Hardtop and Convertible) = 51.6 in. (1311 mm); (Fastback) = 51.8 in. (1316 mm); Luggage space as before but 9.2 cu. ft (260.4 litres) for Hardtop, 5.1 cu. ft (144.3 litres) for Fastback; Approx weight (Hardtop Six) = 2732 lb (1240 kg); (Hardtop V8) = 2920 lb (1326 kg); (Convertible Six) = 2892 lb (1313 kg); (Convertible V8) = 3080 lb (1398 kg); (Fastback Six) = 2759 lb (1253 kg); (Fastback V8) = 2947 lb (1338 kg); Fuel capacity = 17 US gal. (14.16 Imp. gal., 64.35 litres)
COLOUR AND TRIM Choice of 16 body colours and 20 (Hardtop), 16 (Convertible) or 18 (Fastback) all-vinyl trims
STEERING Ratio = 25.4:1 (manual) or 20.3:1 (power)
BRAKES Dual master cylinder with separate lines to front and rear brakes
ENGINES 289/225 now quoted as 9.8:1 compression ratio. Addition of 390 cu in 'Thunderbird' V8, 4.05 in. × 3.78 in. (6391 cc, 102.9 mm × 96 mm), with 10.5:1 compression ratio, 4-barrel carburettor and hydraulic valve lifters, rated at 320 bhp
TRANSMISSIONS Synchro-Smooth (3-speed all-synchro manual); 4-speed, all-synchro close-ratio manual; SelectShift Cruise-O-Matic (3-speed auto with manual override, sequence P-R-N-D-2-1).
With 200/120 Six, Synchro-Smooth is standard and Cruise-O-Matic optional. With 289/200, 289/225 or 390/320 V8s, Synchro-Smooth is standard and 4-speed manual or Cruise-O-Matic are optional. With 289/271 V8, 4-speed manual is standard and Cruise-O-Matic is optional

1968

DIMENSIONS Luggage space (Hardtop) = 9.3 cu. ft (263 litres); (Convertible) = 6.8 cu. ft (192.4 litres) with top down; (Fastback) = 5.6 cu. ft (158.5 litres); Approx weight (Hardtop Six) = 2797 lb (1270 kg); (Hardtop V8) = 2985 lb (1355 kg); (Convertible Six) = 2924 lb (1328 kg); (Convertible V8) = 3112 lb (1413 kg); (Fastback Six) = 2824 lb (1282 kg); (Fastback V8) = 3012 lb (1367 kg)

COLOUR AND TRIM Choice of 16 body colours and 28 all-vinyl trims

ENGINES 200 cu. in. Six now 8.8:1 compression ratio, rated at 115 bhp. Base 289 cu. in. V8 now 8.7:1 compression ratio, rated at 195 bhp. 289/225 and 289/271 V8s discontinued. 390 cu. in. V8 now quoted as 325 bhp. Addition of 302 cu. in. (4.0 in. × 3.0 in.) V8 (4949 cc, 101.6 mm × 76.2 mm) with 10.0:1 compression ratio, 4-barrel carburettor, hydraulic valve lifters and dual exhausts, rated at 230 bhp. Also 427 cu. in. (4.23 in. × 3.78 in.) V8 (6997 cc, 107.4 mm × 96 mm) with 10.9:1 compression ratio, 4-barrel carburettor, hydraulic valve lifters and dual exhausts, rated at 390 bhp. Also (to special order only) 302 cu. in. V8 for racing, with 11.0:1 compression ratio, special induction system, solid valve lifters and dual exhausts, rated at 345 bhp

TRANSMISSIONS As 1967. With 302/230 V8, Synchro-Smooth is standard and Cruise-O-Matic or 4-speed manual are optional. With racing 302/345 V8, 4-speed manual is standard. With 427/390 V8, Cruise-0-Matic is standard

1969

BODY TYPES Hardtop, Convertible, SportsRoof, Mach I and Grandé

DIMENSIONS Wheelbase = 108 in. (2743 mm); Track front and rear = 58.5 in. (1486 mm); Length = 187.4 in. (4760 mm); Width = 71.3 in. (1811 mm); Height = 51.3 in. (1303 mm); Luggage space (Hardtop) = 9.8 cu. ft (277 litres); (Convertible) = 8 cu. ft (226 litres); (SportsRoof) = 5.3 cu. ft (150 litres); Approx weight with six-cylinder engines (Hardtop) = 2832 lb (1286 kg); (Convertible) = 2942 lb (1336 kg); (SportsRoof) = 2856 lb (1297 kg); Fuel capacity = 20 US gal. (16.66 Imp. gal., 75.7 litres)

COLOUR AND TRIM Choice of 16 body colours and 5 standard vinyl trims, 6 optional vinyl trims, 4 cloth and vinyl trims in Grandé, and 3 knitted vinyl trims in Mach I

TYRES Normally C78-14 with 200, 250 and 302 cu. in. engines. E70-14 wide-oval belted white sidewalls on Mach I. Tyre equipment also related to engine power, etc.

ENGINES 289/195 and 427/390 discontinued. New 250 cu. in. (3.68 in. × 3.91 in.) Six (4097 cc, 93.5 mm × 99.3 mm) with 9.0:1 compression ratio, single-barrel carburettor and hydraulic valve lifters, rated at 155 bhp. 302 cu. in. V8 now with 9.5:1 compression ratio and 2-barrel carburettor, rated at 220 bhp. New 351 cu in (4.0 in. × 3.5 in.) V8 (5752 cc, 101.6 mm × 88.9 mm) with 9.5:1 compression ratio and 2-barrel carburettor, rated at 250 bhp. New 351 cu. in. V8 with 10.7:1 compression ratio and 4-barrel carburettor, rated at 290 bhp. 390 cu in V8 now rated at 320 bhp. New 428 (4.13 in. × 3.98 in.) V8 (7014 cc, 104.9 mm × 101.1 mm) with 10.6:1 compression ratio and 4-barrel carburettor, rated at 335 bhp. Alternative 428 cu in Cobra Jet Ram-Air V8, also rated at 335 bhp
TRANSMISSIONS As 1968 but with choice of wide or close ratios for 4-speed manual transmission. With 250/155 V8, 3-speed manual is standard, automatic is optional. With 351 cu. in. engines, 3-speed manual is standard, with option of any other listed transmission. With 428 cu. in. engines, either automatic or wide-ratio 4-speed manual transmission is supplied to choice
GENERAL With 428 cu. in. engines, 80 amp-hr battery

1970

BODY TYPES As 1969 plus Boss 302 and Boss 429
DIMENSIONS Wheelbase = 108 in. (2743 mm); Width = 71.7 in. (1821 mm); Height = 50.6 in. (1285 mm) for SportsRoof, 51.5 in. (1308 mm) for Hardtop and Convertible; Luggage space (Hardtop) = 8.3 cu. ft (235 litres); (Convertible and SportsRoof) = 7.2 cu. ft (183 litres); Approx weight with six-cylinder engines (Hardtop) = 3080 lb (1398 kg); (Convertible) = 3190 lb (1448 kg); (SportsRoof) = 3104 lb (1409 kg). Fuel capacity of California models = 22 US gal. (18.33 Imp. gal., 83.27 litres)
COLOUR AND TRIM Choice of 16 body colours and 6 standard vinyl trims, 6 optional knitted vinyl trims, 5 cloth and vinyl trims in Grandé, plus blazer cloth and vinyl colours
STEERING Overall ratio = 25.45:1 (manual) or 20.48:1 (power)
ENGINES 200 cu. in. Six now rated at 120 bhp. 351 cu. in. V8 with 4-barrel carburetter now quoted as 11:1 compression ratio and rated at 300 bhp. 390/320 V8 discontinued. New 302 cu. in. 'Boss' V8 with 10.6:1 compression ratio and 4-barrel carburettor, rated at 290 bhp. New 429 cu. in. (4.36 in. × 3.60 in.) 'Boss' V8 (7030 cc, 111 mm × 91.4 mm) with 10.5:1 compression ratio, 4-barrel carburettor and solid valve lifters, rated at 375 bhp
TRANSMISSIONS 4-speed manual now supplied with Hurst shifter. With Boss 302, 4-

speed manual is standard (wide or close ratio). With Boss 429, close-ratio 4-speed manual is standard. All other combinations as in 1969 specifications

STANDARD EQUIPMENT (Hardtop) includes colour-keyed carpeting, courtesy lights, lighter, heater/defroster, high-back seats, steering-column lock, printed-circuit instrument panel, aluminized/stainless exhaust system, E78-14 fibreglass-belted bias ply tyres, etc. (Convertible) Hardtop features plus 5-ply vinyl top with colour-keyed cover, full-width rear seat, courtesy lights under dash, etc. (SportsRoof) Hardtop features plus integral tail spoiler, tinted rear window, swing-out rear quarter windows, etc. (Grandé) Hardtop features plus extra sound insulation, luxury trim, moulded door trim panels, de luxe 2-spoke steering wheel, wood-effect instrument panel, electric clock, bright pedal trim, racing mirrors, sidestripes, black or white landau-type vinyl roof covering, houndstooth interior trim, soft-ride suspension, etc. (Mach I) Hardtop features plus simulated bonnet louvres with turn signal telltales, shaker scoop, racing mirrors, wood-effect console, Rim-Blow 3-spoke steering wheel, bonnet lockpins, deep-dish wheel covers with diecast centres, simulated driving lamps, dual exhaust extensions, competition suspension, etc. (Boss) Hardtop/SportsRoof features plus competition suspension with staggered rear shocks, 16:1 steering ratio, F60-15 tyres, spacesaver spare, special cooling package, front spoiler, power-assisted front disc brakes, etc.

Acknowledgements

Probably the most respected freelance motoring writer in the USA, Karl Ludvigsen has also seen the auto industry from the inside as an executive of General Motors, Fiat North America and Ford Europe, and he was the obvious choice to write a Mustang history for *Automobile Quarterly*. Although that project was abandoned, he retained his reference files on the subject, and when I asked his guidance on sources, with amazing but quite typical generosity he allowed me free access to his own material. He also advised me to consult the *A Q* Mustang history which was eventually written by Gary L. Witzenburg, the man he had recommended for the job. It is an exhaustive work which certainly justifies Karl's confidence in its author. Valuable information was also provided readily by *Automobile Quarterly*'s publisher and president, L. Scott Bailey; by David W. Brownell of *Special Interest Autos*; by Stuart Turner and David Burgess Wise of Ford in Britain; and by Dr Paul R. Woudenberg, whose knowledge of automotive history ranges far and wide.

It was Karl Ludvigsen, too, who provided many of the pictures, for his skill as a photographer rivals his writing ability. Scott Bailey helped again by supplying photographs, as did Baron K. Bates of Chrysler Corporation and that every-obliging man, Cyril Posthumus. I must make special mention of the Ford Photographic Unit at South Ockenden, where Sheila Knapman and her colleagues never ceased to be friendly and helpful, however much I asked of them. And it was a red-letter day for me when Jonathan Thompson was kind enough to loan me the picture files of *Road & Track* and *Car Life*, allowing me to use not only a large number of FoMoCo photographs which had proved unobtainable elsewhere, but also some by Dean Batchelor, Beach and Barnes, Boulevard Photographic, Chittenden, Paul Hansen and Henry Manney.

Henry Austin Clark Jr of Long Island, N Y, a man who needs absolutely no introduction to American motoring historians, took the photograph of Alfred E. Donze's 1965 Mustang hardtop which appears on the front cover. As always, my American-born wife Caroline was able to interpret any pieces of transatlantic idiom that defeated a mere Celtic Briton.

Index